The Window
of the Lord's Return

A needed second look
at the rapture and the end times

John Shorey

Copyright © August 2010

Second printing June 2011

Third printing March 2012

Forth printing May 2012

Fifth printing   June 2012

CHECK OUT
www.tribulationtruth.com

Cover photo taken by John Shorey at their Arizona home.

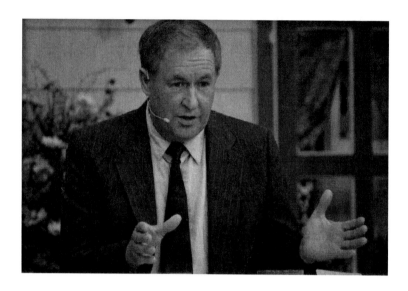

About the Author

My wife Shawnette and I met while attending Northwest Bible College in Kirkland, Washington in 1977. We were married in 1978 and reared two boys who are serving God. Shawnette and I gave most of our service to God by ministering to children. We spent five years traveling across the country as evangelists to children and their families. We also spent many years as children's pastors and currently reside in Arizona. I have sensed God's directing me to write this book, the strongest tug by God's Holy Spirit that I have ever experienced. In an attitude of obedience, I have been diligent to complete this assignment.

Always in His Service,

John Shorey

I have known John Shorey since 1974 and have always observed his very careful and considerate study of the Word of God; therefore, I feel sure that this venture into the subject of the prophetic future is accompanied by much prayer and careful study of God's Word. It is a task most men would try to avoid, for the task is awesome, and the message often is rejected by the rank and file of Christianity.

Based upon the serious situations simmering in our world, his writings make a person examine one's beliefs and some teachings in this light, in order to determine to be all God would have one to be as the time-clock moves closer to midnight.

May we determine to have oil in our lamps, trimmed and shining brightly, until that day.

Reverend Jack and Betty Bransford
Retired pastors and former Alaska District Superintendent of the Assembly of God

I would like to thank a few of those who have continued with me as I have worked on this study. Those who gave me their opinions and encouragement were:

Betty Bransford, Ron LaVoie, Jerry Logue, and Chuck Lorentzen,

A special thanks to Ron LaVoie, my computer technician.

A special thanks to a team of helpers, who stepped up to the plate and helped me with the huge job of editing this book. Thank you, Robert Casey, Lottie Holland, Ivan Secord and Greg Foster.

Tyler Rasmussen, Graphic Designer

This book is published by Instantpublisher.com

The Window of the Lord's Return

Introduction

When I think about the title of this book, <u>The Window of the Lord's Return</u>, I think about the future window of time of the Lord's return. It is my conviction that when Israel became a nation in 1948, a time-clock was started, and this generation will not pass away until the return of the Lord Jesus. Recently, I heard Reverend John Hagee say that we are the Terminal Generation. I believe he meant that this generation will live to see the coming of the Lord. Since 1948, sixty-four years of this generation have expired. In chapter eleven of this book, I will present a strong argument for my position that seventy years is the length of a generation.

Some will ask, "Where do you see the Bible teach that Israel would be restored as a nation in the last days?" First we need to look at Ezekiel 36:24, (KJV) *"For I will take you from among the heathen, and gather you out of all countries, and will bring you into your own land."* Then look at Matthew 24:32-34, (NIV). *"Learn this lesson from the fig tree: As soon as its twigs get tender and its leaves come out, you know that summer is near. Even so, when you see all these things, you know that it is near, right at the door. I tell you the truth; this generation will certainly not pass away until all these things have happened."* The reference to the fig tree is referring to the nation of Israel, and figs refer to the people of Israel. I will show Bible references to support this teaching. The following verses in Joel 1:6-7, (KJV), shows that Israel, the land that belongs to God will be laid waste. This land is described as the fig tree, a fig tree that died.

"For a nation is come upon my land, strong and without number, whose teeth are the teeth of a lion, and he hath the cheek teeth of a great lion. He hath laid my vine waste and barked my fig tree: he hath made it clean bare, and cast it away: the branches thereof are made white."

The next verse I will use will show that the people of Israel were referred to as figs. They would be judged and removed from their land and dispersed around the world in judgment from God. Jeremiah 24:8-9, (KJV), *"And as the evil figs, which cannot be eaten, they are so evil; surely thus saith the LORD, So will I give Zedekiah the king of Judah, and his princes, and the residue of Jerusalem, that remain in this land, and them that dwell in the land of Egypt: And I will deliver them to be removed into all the kingdoms of the earth for their hurt, to be a reproach and a proverb, a taunt and a curse, in all the places whither I shall drive them."*

In 1948 the Children of Israel were allowed to return to the land of Israel. Note in Matthew 24:32: "When you see the branches get tender and its leaves come out," this is refering to life coming back to the fig tree or Israel, which was fulfilled in 1948. When you look at Joel 1:6-7, (above) you see that when the nation of Israel was brought back to life, it was referred to as the fig tree. This Land is also referred to as the land that belongs to God, also called Israel.

In this study, I will be looking at this narrowing window of time and attempt to show how close we are to the Lord's return. I will also be sharing an in-depth study on the rapture and other related end-time subjects. One of the subjects that I will be covering is the timing of the rapture in relation to the Great Tribulation. I realize that this is a sensitive subject for many. Please realize that the timing of the rapture has no bearing on our salvation, but it is important that we get it right.

I was reared mostly in the Catholic Church (my mother's choice) where I never heard anything about end-time doctrines. My father came from a large protestant Christian family. It was from his family that I was first exposed to end-times doctrines. When I became a Christian in 1974, the church was all abuzz about the second coming and imminent return of Jesus Christ. So, early in my new Christian walk, the rapture doctrine and the Book of Revelation caught my attention and has been an area of interest throughout my Christian life. I have heard some great preaching on the subject, mostly years ago. It is interesting, now that we are so close to the return of Christ, you do not seem to hear as much preaching on the subject. Why is that? Could it be that many prophets of our time have been wrong, and sayings like, "You are as slow as the second coming", has made some steer away from this important end-time teaching? Could it be that some think that end-time events are too negative a subject and that the church is so caught up in the things of the world and keeping up with the Jones that we do not want to hear this message that would disrupt our lives?

I have studied this subject intently over the years and have come up with some interesting thoughts. With current events as they are, I am seeing so many of these thoughts coming together. I feel God's direction to share them with others, as I believe God is trying to tell us something. I am convinced that we do not want to get caught unprepared for these coming events.

What I have done is separate these thoughts into a few separate discussions, and you can decide if they all fit together.

During the three years that I have been working on this book, I would send off portions to friends seeking their opinions. I have been looking for answers, so when I ask someone to look this over, it is usually someone I highly respect. Some comments have been shallow, but the majority has been very positive.

Years ago, I had some incredible opportunities to witness to many high-up Mormon leaders. I will not go into the total who's who, but one invitation was from an astronaut who landed on the moon. This took place while I was attending the University of Alaska, in Fairbanks. On another occasion I was meeting with the ward president and former ward president of the Ketchikan, Alaska, Mormon Church. I was trying to show them proof that the Book of Mormon originated from a plagiarized work of a minister who wrote the story from where the Book of Mormon originated, before it came into the hands of Joseph Smith. I had the proof of handwriting experts, and I was ready to show these two men, but they refused to look at the evidence because they did not want to see something different from what they had been taught.

In light of our tendency to have a similar attitude, let us consider that the Bible admonishes us to, "Study to show thyself approved unto God, a workman that needeth not to be ashamed, rightly dividing the word of truth" 2 Timothy 2:15 (KJV). It is interesting what is said in Daniel, *"...the truth of this prophecy would be sealed until the time of the end...".* So since we have been trying to explain this prophecy for hundreds of years, could it be possible that we have made mistakes? Is studying and rightly dividing the word of truth concerning the prophecy of the end-times important enough to take a serious second look at from time to time? I believe it is.

Table of contents

1. Could we be wrong about a Pre-Tribulation rapture?

Could it be possible that many mainstream churches have taken a doctrinal position for their churches - a doctrine on the second coming and the imminent return of Christ that was based on incomplete information and poor interpretation of Scripture?

I do not understand why it is so hard to accept the fact that we do not always get our theology right. Throughout church history, time has had a way of revealing the truth and correcting our errors. Based on what Jesus said about John, Jesus' disciples thought that Jesus would return in their lifetime. All but one of Jesus' disciples were martyred and they were wrong about the timing of Christ's return.

Then replacement theology came along, it taught that the nation of Israel was rejected by God and was replaced by the church; therefore, Israel did not have to be reborn as a nation. Again they were wrong.

Then almost two hundred years ago John Darby had a revelation that said that Christ would return for his bride before the seven year Great Tribulation started. His teaching along with the dream of a teenage girl, switched the church from a mid-Tribulation view of the rapture to a pre-Tribulation view. If you will do a study on the internet, on the history of the pre-Tribulation view of the rapture, you will see it was cloaked in confusion and disagreement. Over time, this change in doctrine was accepted; because, it sounded good and made people feel comfortable. Just because a doctrine sounds good does not make it right.

What I have discovered in sharing the first printing of this book with pastors is that many pastors are not open to the possibility that they have believed a doctrine on Christ's coming that could be flawed. Sid Roth wrote a book called, They Thought for Themselves. This book is about Jews who have discovered Jesus as their Lord; because, they thought for themselves. It is interesting the reaction I get from lay Christians who are students of the Word and have an open mind to read this study. I hear comments like the following all the time: "I read it twice, I looked up the Bible verses, I believe you are right, and I just cannot believe we didn't see it." A friend I went to college with told me, "John, when I saw where you were going with the mid-Tribulation view of the rapture, I did not want you to be right, but after I studied your position, I have to say, I believe you are right." **One Christian leader told me. "If anyone would read your book with an open mind, they will get it. The case for the mid-Tribulation rapture is so plain in your book."**

When I went to Bible College, one of the top doctrinal professors told us that the rapture doctrine is most popular in America. In many parts of the world, Christians have suffered and are suffering persecution, hunger, and martyrdom on a daily basis. It is interesting that American Christians believe so strongly that God would never allow his people to suffer and go through tribulation. We have lost sight of the fact that in the early church, many of Christ's disciples were martyred. We should all read the book, Foxe's Book of Martyrs. We would realize that when the church was standing up to persecution, the fruit of their lives was the salvation of souls.

Could the church be wrong about the timing of the rapture, and what would be the ramifications of this mistake? Please do not be offended if my conclusions fly totally contrary to what most Christian churches believe. I have been explor-

2

ing this question from the beginning of this study, and I am seeing too many Scriptures that do not add up, building a strong case that we will not see a pre-Tribulation rapture.

I really would like someone to show me why I am wrong in my interpretation; because, I would much rather see a pre-Tribulation rapture as opposed to having to go through part of the Great Tribulation. One question that has to be asked; "Is it possible to misread God's word and have a belief system based on the poor interpretation of God's Word?"

Here is an example from John 14:2-3, (KJV): *"In my Father's house are many mansions; if it were not so, I would have told you. I go to prepare a place for you and if I go and prepare a place for you, I will come again and receive you to myself, that where I am, there you may be also."*

Many Christians read this and believe that we will all have a mansion in heaven. In fact, hymns and songs have been written, enforcing this belief. If you read this verse carefully, you will see that this verse does not say that we will all have a mansion. What it says is, *"In my Father's house are MANY mansions..."* Many mansions does not mean that all places in heaven are mansions. In Hollywood, there are many mansions, but all homes in that area are not mansions. The Word goes on to say *"...I go to prepare a place for you..."* The key word here is 'PLACE'. A place could be a tent and a cot. Does not God's word teach us that we can lay up treasures in heaven? It is similar to having a heavenly bank account. Does not the word say that only what is done for Christ will last? If your place in heaven is based on your heavenly bank account, do you believe you will have a mansion or a tent waiting for you?

If you are still not convinced that we will not all have a mansion in heaven you should read, 1Corinthians 3:12-15, (NIV): *"For no one can lay any foundation other than the*

3

one already laid, which is Jesus Christ. If any man builds on this foundation using gold, silver, costly stones, wood, hay, or straw, his work will be shown for what it is, because the Day will bring it to light. It will be revealed with fire, and the fire will test the quality of each man's work. If what he has built survives, he will receive his reward. If it is burned up, he will suffer loss, he himself will be saved, but only as one escaping through the flames."

I have received some comments, saying that I should not burst people's bubble, but I should only teach words of comfort. I am sorry, but I disagree. I feel too many preachers have watered down their preaching instead of being honest with their flock. When we arrive in eternity would you want to be found guilty of holding back the truth? People need to realize that only what's done for Christ will count. Life is short, and we need to be sure we are burning our candle for God.

I believe the most important book we should ever read is the Bible, inspired and breathed into his chosen writers to deliver the Word of God to man. I believe a mistake we can make is to take the writings and teachings of man as gospel-truth, instead of checking these teachings against the Word of God. In the New Testament, during the time of Paul, when he was preaching to the Bereans, Paul gave us a good example to follow. Acts 17:11, (NIV): *"Now the Bereans were of more noble character than the Thessalonians, for they received the message with great eagerness and examined the Scriptures every day to see if what Paul said was true."*

A book I recently read is a good example of why we need to examine what we read against what God's Word says. It is entitled, <u>The Rapture and What We Should Do Until Christ Returns,</u> by Reverend David Obadiah,(not his real name). In his chapter on the rapture of the church, he says

4

that 2 Thessalonians assures its readers that no saint will experience the seven- year Great Tribulation. Reverend Obadiah does not quote chapter and verse to back up this statement. After reading 2 Thessalonians, I could not find any verse to back up this statement. We need to be like the Bereans, who search the Scriptures to see if the Word of God backs up what our Bible teachers are telling us. Please do not question my motives for using real examples. Reverend David Obadiah is a great teacher, but I am finding that even great teachers can be wrong in their interpretations of the Bible. I am sure that I will have mistakes pointed out to me as well.

As I mentioned at the beginning of these writings, I have always had a keen interest in prophecy and end-time teachings, much of which have come from the Book of Revelation. I have always enjoyed reading Revelation and have always been spurred on to read more of Revelation from the admonition given in Revelation 1:3 (NIV): *"Blessed is the one who reads the words of this prophecy, and blessed are those who hear it and take to heart what is written in it, because the time is near."*

As I have read the book of Revelation over the years, from the time that I was a new Christian, at times it seems it has generated more questions than answers. I have always believed that as we approach the time of the Lord's coming, our questions would be made plain to us. Over the years, I have read many of the classic books on the end-times. But as I look at Revelation in light of what has been happening in the last few years, I am seeing events coming together that make total sense. These events were never thought about thirty years ago when I was only a few years old in the Lord. Thirty years ago, who would have imagined the problems we are having with the Muslim nations and terrorists today. How could we have thought that the Muslim countries would hate America and want to see us destroyed so that we would not stand in the way of the Muslim nation's ultimate goal of destroying Israel? Today things are becoming so clear that I believe we need to revisit how we connect the dots to help us understand how the end-times puzzle fits together.

To start off, I will examine the question: "Could we be wrong about a pre-Tribulation rapture?" I will start off by looking at the beginning of the Great Tribulation, and as we move along, I will bring us back to the key Scriptures for the pre-Tribulation rapture.

When does the Great Tribulation start? This is easy for my discussion, as it seems that many are in agreement with the Great Tribulation starting with the antichrist establishing a seven year peace treaty with Israel and the Muslim nations, as mentioned in the book of Daniel. This event cannot happen until the antichrist is revealed. I believe the antichrist is revealed close to the opening of the first seal of the seven seals found in chapter 6 of the book of Revelation.

The opening of the first seal will reveal events that will take place close to the beginning of the Great Tribulation. I will be showing from God's Word why the events that mark the beginning of the wrath of God will not occur until the trumpet judgments and the bowls of God's wrath later in the Great Tribulation. As I have studied for this book, I have learned that many believe that the wrath of God starts with the four horses at the opening of the seals. I will address this in greater detail later in this study, showing why I believe that the seals are not part of God's wrath. So for the sake of setting up my later discussion, I will bring you through the opening of the seals.

I will show my readers why I believe the Bible teaches the seals represent events during the beginning of the Great Tribulation that are not the wrath of God that is yet to come. One reason that points to the seals as representing events happening during the Great Tribulation that are not the outpouring of God's wrath is that the fifth seal is the martyrdom of the saints. It is not God's doing this to his saints.

A second reason why I do not believe that the opening of the seals represents the wrath of God is that God promised his saints that we would not be accounted for the wrath to come. If you carefully read Revelation 5:2 (NIV), it says, *"And I saw a mighty angel proclaiming in a loud voice, 'Who is worthy to break the seals and open the scroll?' But no one in heaven or on earth or under the earth could open the scroll or even look inside it."* As you read this, you see that there was a message in the opening of each seal, but it is the <u>scroll</u> that contains the wrath of God. The seals are only the locks that are opened by the Lamb, to reveal what is contained inside the scroll.

The Lamb opened the first seal in Revelation 6:1. Here, it talks of a white horse, and its rider held a bow. This is seen as a false christ coming. I believe this is the revealing of the antichrist. We have seen false christ's for generations, but this one is riding a white horse, imitating Christ. He has a bow and no arrows are mentioned, for he is only an imitator without the power. My chapter on the coming antichrist is very insightful and will help in understanding this seal.

The second seal is a red horse whose rider is to take peace from the earth, and wars will be happening all over the earth. This will be far worse than wars and rumors of wars. I believe we will see many wars breaking out throughout the earth to mark this event, yet these wars are not the ones to come at the end of the seven-year time of the Great Tribulation. Later I will discuss some thoughts I have on which nations I believe will be part of this seal.

The third seal talks about a black horse. It says that its rider will hold a pair of scales and is saying, *"A quart of wheat for a day's wages."* This is talking about global famine. And this famine will result in the starvation of millions. Economists are saying that hyper-inflation is coming. It is no longer a question of if, but when it will hit our dollar. It has been said that 2009 was a year of many crop failures in America. We in America have been used to having all the food we need just a few minutes away at the local grocery store. In America, we have had our silos full of wheat and other food commodities for years. What I have recently learned is that our back-up reserves have been disappearing, much being sold to China and Russia. China, a country that has been content to live on a bowl of rice, is now expanding their diet as their economy has expanded.

The year 2010 has dealt even more crop and food failures. A drought in Russia has destroyed twenty-five percent of their wheat crops, and they cut off all exports of wheat in 2010. Russia is the world's largest exporter of wheat. When the seals start to open, and food shortages start to emerge, it will cause food panics unlike anything we have ever seen in America. It will lead to rapid inflation and rationing to try to keep food on store shelves. Ultimately, this will lead to a system of rationing that will require you to accept the anti-christ system in order to buy your food.

The fourth seal was Death followed by Hades, revealed as a rider on a pale horse. It says that he was given power over a fourth of the earth to bring death by war, famine, plague, and wild beasts. I believe that the plagues could be the work of terrorists using biological weapons to bring plagues and death to those whom this event is describing. It may also be possible that the plagues could be epidemics from viruses like Sars or the Swine flu. I have heard some say that this seal will lead to the death of one quarter of the inhabitants on the earth, but if you read this carefully, you will realize it is saying that it will effect one quarter of the earth geographically. It does not say that all will die in this one quarter of the earth. Later, I will explain which countries could be involved. Three of these countries comprise about one quarter of the earth.

The fifth seal talks about Christians who are slain for their testimony of Christ during this part of the Great Tribulation. Read the following from Revelation 6:9-11 (NIV): *"When he opened the fifth seal, I saw under the altar, the souls of those who had been slain because of the word of God and the testimony they had maintained. They called out in a loud voice, 'How long, Sovereign Lord, holy and true, until you judge the inhabitants of the earth and avenge our blood?' "Then each of them was given a white robe, and they were told to wait a little longer, until the number of their fellow servants and brothers who were to be killed as they had been, was completed."*

These are interesting verses to think about. These are Christians killed for staying true to God under the rule of the antichrist. One point to note is that they are under the altar, not at the throne. They are being told to wait for others who are to be killed, for they were to join them. Remember this phrase, "under the altar". It will be important later in this study. Also, note that those who are being killed for their testimony for Christ are asking God, *"How long, Sovereign Lord, holy and true, until you judge the inhabitants of the earth and avenge our blood?"* They could only ask this question if the wrath of God had not yet started. I will be showing more reasons later that add evidence to why the wrath of God does not start until Revelation, chapter 8.

The sixth seal describes events happening in the heavens with the sun and the moon being affected. It says that the sun would be turned black and the moon would be blood-red. It talks about great earthquakes affecting the whole earth. I will cover this seal in greater detail later in this study. I believe that a cataclysmic event has been waiting to happen, that could fulfill this seal.

Now something interesting happens during a break before the seventh seal is opened. In fact, all of chapter 7 takes place and it is not until chapter 8 that the seventh seal is opened. When the seventh seal is opened at the beginning of chapter 8, it says that when he opened the seal, there was silence in heaven for about half an hour, and the seventh seal was left a mystery.

What I want to do is go back and look at what happened in chapter 7. I have read other writers of prophecy talk about this as being an interlude during which millions of souls would be reached with the Gospel. This is the time the 144,000 Jews will be sealed to go out and take the Gospel and salvation knowledge of Christ to the Jews. I have heard over the years a time was coming when the time of the Gentiles would be over and the dispensation for the revealing of Christ to the Jews would begin. At this time, I want to show you some events that are happening in Revelation, chapter 7, about which I have some interesting thoughts.

The first observation I have made about the events of this chapter is, if this is the time of the sealing of the 144,000 Jewish evangelists, then would it not make sense this is the beginning of the dispensation of the salvation of the Jews? And would it also make sense that at about this time, it would be the end of the time of the Gentiles? As I discuss later in this study, I believe a great ingathering of Jews will occur at this time, just before the rapture of God's elect.

It is at this time I want to look for the Scripture verses that talk about the rapture of the believers. It seems to be a consensus among prophetic teachers in the pre-Tribulation camp, that Revelation 4:1 describes the rapture. Jack Van

Impe and many other teachers of a pre-Tribulation rapture use this verse to denote the rapture of the church. Before we go back and look at this verse, I want to show you an event that happens in chapter 7, after the sealing of the 144,000 Jews.

Start reading Revelation 7:9-12 (NIV): *"After this I looked and there before me was a great multitude that no one could count, from every nation, tribe, people and language, standing before the throne and in front of the Lamb. They were wearing white robes and were holding palm branches in their hands. And they cried out in a loud voice: 'Salvation belongs to our God, who sits on the throne, and to the Lamb.' All the angels were standing around the throne and around the elders and the four living creatures. They fell down on their faces before the throne and worshiped God, saying, Amen! Praise and glory and wisdom and thanks and honor and power and strength be to our God for ever and ever, Amen!"* Look at Verse 9. It says, *"a great multitude from every nation, tribe, people and language, standing before the throne."* Now go down to verse 13, and hear what one of the elders who was at the throne has to say about this. "Then one of the elders asked me, 'These in white robes -- who are they, and where did they come from?"

Now, get the picture? One of the elders, who day and night is around the throne of God, suddenly notices a great multitude of uncountable Christians standing around the throne worshiping God. He acts as if he did not know from where they came. Then he answers his own question. Listen to the answer in verse 14. "I answered, 'Sir, you know.' And he said, "These are they who have come out of the Great Tribulation; they have washed their robes and made them white in the blood of the Lamb."

My question is, "If this great multitude just now showed up in heaven after the sixth seal, and the rapture happened in Revelation 4:1 before the Great Tribulation started, then who are these who just showed up?" Is there a second rapture for the tribulation saints? I do not see that as scriptural. To me, what we are seeing here is the church going through part of the Great Tribulation until it gets to the part where the 144,000 Jews are sealed to be God's chosen messengers to start preaching and revealing the love of Christ to the Jewish nation. I believe the 144,000 Jewish evangelists will bring many Jews to Christ just in time for the rapture of the bride of Christ.

One argument I have heard against what I just said is that this is a second rapture for the Jews. One big problem with this explanation is, "Why would you have a separate rapture of the Jews, when all Jews who accept Christ will go up in the rapture anyway". Besides, the two witnesses who play a part in God's dealing with the Jews are not even yet mentioned. They are to witness to the Jewish nation for three and a half years during the second half of the Great Tribulation. So how can Revelation 7:14 be talking about a second rapture of the Jews? Also, when you read Revelation 7:9, it says these people who have just appeared in heaven came from every nation, tribe, people, and language.

The same argument is used that these are Jews, who are living in every nation and speak in every language. However, this verse says, "Every people, nation and language". This verse ties into another verse, and this gets very exciting. Look at Revelation 5:9 (NIV). This is where only Jesus was qualified to open the seals, and it says, *"You are worthy to take the scroll and to open its seals, because you were slain, and with your blood you purchased men for God from every tribe, language, people, and nation."* THIS IS ME AND YOU THAT ARE BEING TALKED

12

ABOUT; THIS IS THE CHURCH THAT CHRIST RE-DEEMED WITH HIS BLOOD. Now look at Revelation 7:9 (NIV), and you will see Christ collecting in the rapture what he has already purchased! *"After this I looked, and there before me was a great multitude that no one could count, from every NATION, TRIBE, PEOPLE, and LAN-GUAGE. Standing before the throne and in front of the Lamb."*

Please pay close attention to what I am going to show you.
I want to take you back to an event that lies between Revelation 4:1 and Revelation 7:11-14. Remember, Revelation 4:1, is the pre-Tribulation verse for when the rapture takes place. Look at Revelation 5:11-12 (KJV): *"And I beheld, and I heard the voice of many angels around the throne and the beasts and the elders: and the number of them was ten thousand times ten thousand and thousands of thousands; Saying with a loud voice, 'Worthy is the Lamb that was slain to receive power and riches and wisdom and strength, and honor and glory and blessing."* **Look at who are described as being around the throne. It is angels, beasts, and elders, but there is no mention of <u>saints</u> around the throne. If the saints were raptured in Revelation 4:1, they would be around the throne in white robes in this passage.**

Now when you read Revelation 7:11-14, you hear the elder, who is always around the throne, asking, "Who are these multitudes that no one can number in white robes..." Who have suddenly shown up? The elder then reflects, and he says that they are those who have come out of the Great Tribulation. **Now stop right here and think about this. If the rapture had already happened pre-Tribulation in Revelation 4:1, then the millions of pre-Tribulation Christians would have been in white robes around the throne in both Revelation chapter 5 and chapter 7. They would have blended in with the multitude that the elder**

was asking about in Revelation 7:11-14. Do you think there are two raptures? No. I do not see this in the Word of God. These verses show the rapture just did not happen in Revelation 4:1.

Next, I would like you to go to 1 Thessalonians 4:15-18. This Scripture shows why the rapture could not have happened until after Revelation 5:11-12. Read 1 Thessalonians 4:15-18 (KJV): *"For this we say unto you by the word of the Lord, that we which are alive and remain unto the coming of the Lord shall not prevent them which are asleep. For the Lord himself shall descend from heaven with a shout, with the voice of the archangel, and with the trump of God: and the dead in Christ will rise first: Then we which are alive and remain shall be caught up together with them in the clouds, to meet the Lord in the air: and so shall we ever be with the Lord. Wherefore comfort one another with these words."*

This Scriptures show why the rapture could not have happened until after Revelation 5:11-12. Read 1 Thessalonians 4:17. It says that both the dead in Christ and those who are alive will both be raptured together to meet the Lord in the air, and then it says that we shall ever be with the Lord. If, from the point of the rapture, we will forever be with the Lord, then think about it, if we will be with the Lord, then we would be with the Lord in Revelation 5:11-12, around the throne. But if there is no mention of saints in white robes around the throne in Revelation 5:11-12, then the rapture has not yet happened. So when the elder in Revelation 7:9 and 13 (NIV) asks who the multitudes in white robes are, which no man can number, he is told that they are the saints who have come out of the Great Tribulation. Revelation 7:9 (NIV), *"After this I looked and there before me was a great multitude that no one could count, from every nation, tribe, people, and language standing before the throne and in front of the Lamb. They were hold-*

14

ing palm branches in their hands." Can it be any clearer? The rapture, the only rapture, has just taken place according to Revelation 7:9.

Martyred Saints Show the Timing of the Rapture

One argument I get is that these saints who suddenly appeared around the throne are martyred saints who are coming out of the Great Tribulation, as they are being killed for not taking the mark of the beast. I want you to think about this as I share why this could not be the case. To begin with, this event around the throne happens in an instant, proven by the fact that the elder who is asking the question is always at the throne. It is like he blinked, and suddenly there were millions in white robes around the throne. This would mean, if they were the Great Tribulation martyred saints, they would have had to have been killed at the same time. I do not think this is possible. Also, there is a second problem with this opinion. When the saints are being martyred, as described in the fifth seal in Revelation 6:9, it says the martyred saints are under the altar and not at the throne. Also, they are asking in, Revelation 6:10-11, (NIV*), "How long, Sovereign Lord, holy and true, until you judge the inhabitants of the earth and avenge our blood?" 'Then each of them was given a white robe, and they were told to wait a little longer, until the number of their fellow servants and brothers who were to be killed as they had been was completed. "*

Then it says they were each given white robes. Notice, they are still under the altar, not at the throne! If these martyred saints were at the throne in Revelation 6:10, in the white robes that they were given while under the altar, then the elder in Revelation 7 would not have even noticed a second multitude showing up. For over the last 2000 years, millions of Christians have been martyred. At the point of the rapture, they would all have <u>been</u> at the throne. **Now think about this, if all the martyred saints of all time do not show up at the throne until Revelation 7:9, then how can you say the rapture happened in Revelation 4:1?**

Now let us go back and look at Revelation 4:1, which is considered the pre-Tribulation rapture verse. *"After this I looked, and there before me was a door standing open in heaven. And the voice I had first heard speaking to me like a trumpet said, 'Come up here, and I will show you what must take place after this.' At once I was in the Spirit, and there before me was the throne in heaven with someone sitting on it."*

I just do not see the rapture in Revelation 4:1. What I do see is John, the Revelator, being taken to heaven to the very throne of God where God tells him, *"...I will show you what must take place after this."* Paul had a similar experience when Christ was revealing revelations to him. Then, if you will go to Revelation 19:11, you will see the heavens opened up again, just like what happened in Revelation 4:1. Read, Revelation 19:11, (NIV): *"I saw heaven standing open, and there before me was a white horse, whose rider is called Faithful and True. With justice he judges and makes war."* This is a revelation of Christ after the battles have been won and the marriage supper of the Lamb is about to take place. This heaven standing open does not mean a gateway is open for a rapture event; because, if you will go back to Revelation 19:6-8, you will see that the saints are already <u>in</u> heaven about to celebrate with Christ at the marriage supper of the Lamb. Read Revelation 19:6-8 (NIV*): "Then I heard what sounded like a great multitude, like the roar of rushing waters, and like loud peals of thunder, shouting: 'Hallelujah! For our Lord God Almighty reigns. Let us rejoice and be glad and give him glory! For the wedding of the Lamb has come, and his bride has made* *herself ready. Fine linen, bright and clean, was given her to wear."*

I would like to know where there is a second or third Scripture that shows the timing of the rapture as being pre-Tribulation. I was taught in Bible school that doctrine has to be backed with the witness of two or three scriptures. You might ask, "Where do I see two or more scriptures to support the rapture as happening after the opening of the six seals in Revelation 6?" I have already shown you a number of verses in Revelation that show the rapture happening after the opening of the seals during the Great Tribulation. Now I want to show you from the Gospels where I see three places that describe almost verbatim what is happening in the opening of the seven seals of Revelation 6. All three describe what I believe is the rapture happening after the opening of the sixth seal.

If you will go to Matthew 24:4-5, (NIV): *"Jesus answered: "Watch out that no one deceives you. For many will come in my name claiming, 'I am the Christ', and will deceive many."* This verse coincides with the first seal about false christs.

Matthew 24:7a, (NIV): *"Nation will rise against nation, and kingdom against kingdom."* This coincides with the second seal.

Matthew 24:7b, (NIV): *"There will be famines and earthquakes in various places."* This coincides with the third seal.

Matthew 24:9, (NIV): *"Then you will be handed over to be persecuted and put to death, and you will be hated by all nations because of me."* This coincides with the fifth seal.

17

Matthew 24:29, (NIV): *"the sun will be darkened, and the moon will not give its light, the stars will fall from the sky, and the heavenly bodies will be shaken."* This coincides with the sixth seal.

Now read Matthew 24:30-31, (NIV): *"At that time, the sign of the Son of Man will appear in the sky, and all the nations of the earth will mourn. They will see the Son of Man coming on the clouds of the sky, with power and great glory. And he will send his angels with a loud trumpet call, and they will gather his elect from the four winds, from one end of the heavens to the other."* Am I taking this wrong? I do not think so, this sounds like the rapture. Look at Mark 13:6-27, and you will see a similar parallel. Then look at Luke 21:8-27, and you will see another.

One of the established arguments for the pre-Tribulation rapture is conjecture from Revelation 4:1. Some teachers are saying that the church is not mentioned after Revelation 4:1. I do not see this as true, for it says the saints would be martyred during the fifth seal of the Great Tribulation in Revelation 6. Again, in Revelation 14:11-13, it talks of those who are taking the mark of the beast and the needed patience of the saints. During this time, it goes on to say many saints will be martyred. Now I know there are some who teach that those are Tribulation saints. Tell me, where are the words "Tribulation saints" found in the Bible? Realize, we are setting the time of the rapture as a pre-Tribulation event, not based on Scripture verses, but based on the omission of the word "church" after Revelation 4:1. As I see it, the timing of the rapture is too important to establish this doctrine without Scripture, chapter, and verse to back up this position. **Plus, think about this: what is the church? It is the saints that make the church, so if the saints are mentioned after Revelation 4:1, then the church is mentioned. Later in chapter eight I do a study**

on the church, and what I found really strengthens what I am saying here.

In closing, I want to pose the question that some will ask, "Is it really that important as to when the rapture happens? Should not we just be ready?" This is a good question. The problem I see is, if the churches are teaching the rapture will come before the Great Tribulation, then this gives the church a false sense of security. I have heard pastors say God would not allow his church to go through suffering. Yet as I mentioned above, in Revelation 14:11-13, it says that the saints will have to have patient endurance during the Great Tribulation when the antichrist is pushing his system of the mark of the beast. If the saints, who have expected the pre-Tribulation rapture are all of a sudden seeing themselves in the Great Tribulation without warning and no time to get ready for this turbulent time, I believe it will cause many Christians to turn away from God. They may start believing that they have been abandoned by God, and I believe it will lead to many accepting the system of the antichrist rather than starve to death. I believe that the events happening today, with the world economies on the verge of collapse, are setting the world stage to cause the world populations to look for a savior in the form of the antichrist. We, as believers, need to be the ones who are looking for the signs of Christ's coming and prepare for the tribulation of these times, as Joseph did. When the hard times come, we will be able to take care of the needs of our families and others. We will be in a position to be used by God for the greatest revival the world has ever seen.

Before moving to the next section, I want to add some thoughts that will answer questions I often hear when this Bible verse is referenced: 1 Thessalonians 1:10, (KJV): *"Even Jesus, which delivered us from the wrath to come"*. This text is often taken to mean that the rapture of the church will be a pre-Tribulation event in order to spare the

19

church from the wrath of the Great Tribulation, but the Bible calls the time period leading up to the return of Christ "the Great Tribulation", a seven-year period that will become more and more intense as we get closer to Christ's second coming.

If you look at the beginning of the Great Tribulation and the opening of the seven seals, you will see events that are similar to what has happened for all of time: wars, earthquakes, and famine, and even the martyrdom of the saints, which is the fifth seal. Just like a woman's labor pains grow in intensity as the time of the delivery of her child approaches, it will be the same growth of intensity when the seals are opened at the beginning of the Great Tribulation. The intensity of wars will be higher, earthquakes will be more devastating, and famines will be more widespread.

Most Christians who hold to the pre-Tribulation rapture believe we will miss out on the seals and all of the Great Tribulation. Many people refer to 1 Thessalonians 1:10, (KJV): *"And to wait for his Son from heaven, whom he raised from the dead, even Jesus, which delivered us from the wrath to come."* If you look closely at this verse, it says that we will be delivered from the wrath to come. This means the "wrath of God". This verse does not say that we will be delivered from tribulation to come. In fact, think about it, the Great Tribulation is not called the Great Wrath of God. When the seals are being opened, I do not see the evidence in God's Word that shows the seals are the wrath of God. God does not start wars, create famine, and certainly does not martyr his saints as described in the fifth seal. The wrath of God does not start until Revelation 8-9 and then picks up again in chapter 15.

We need to understand what the Bible teaches about tribulation. The Bible says tribulation works patience. During the Great Tribulation, it is interesting that during the time

20

that the saints are battling with the antichrist, God's word tells us in Revelation 13:10, (NIV): *"If anyone is to go into captivity, into captivity he will go. If anyone is to be killed with the sword, he will be killed. This calls for patient endurance on the part of the saints."* I believe this passage of text is teaching us that the saints will be going through a period of tribulation that will lead to a great revival and at the same time bring about a purification of the church. Does the Bible not teach us that Christ is coming back for a pure bride worthy of being called the bride of Christ?

Many churches today are caught up in entertaining both the saved and the lost, believing that great performances will make people feel good and so draw them closer to God. I believe if we would put a greater effort into ministering to the needs of the hurting, we would see a greater maturity in our churches and a greater harvest of the lost.

The Bible teaches in these last days we will see the birth pains increasing preceding Christ's coming that will turn people's lives upside down. As God allows economic and natural disasters on the earth, Christians may ask, "What are you doing, God?" I imagine God's answer to this question would be, "I'm not trying to make you feel good, I'm trying to wake you up and draw you closer to Me."

I was recently reading a book, The Best of A. W. Tozer. He was a great preacher of a previous generation, and he made a profound statement in the chapter, "Why we are lukewarm about Christ's return". **"History reveals that times of suffering for the church have also been times of looking upward. Tribulation has always sobered God's people and encouraged them to look for and yearn after the return of the Lord. Our present preoccupation with this world may be a warning of bitter days to come. God will wean us from the earth someway—the easy way if possible, the hard way if necessary. It's up to us."**

2. The sealing of the 144,000 and other pre-rapture events

As I have studied the book of Revelation, I have noticed that the 144,000 Jews were mentioned in chapter 7 and again in chapter 14. In chapter 7, the sealing of these Jews happens just before that which I am convinced is the time of the rapture of the church. As it says in Revelation 7:9 (NIV): *"After this, I looked and there before me was a great multitude that no one could count..."* Now, if you look at Revelation 14, you will see the mentioning of the 144,000 again, and as you continue reading Revelation 14:14-19, you will see what appears to be Jesus Christ in the clouds. Then in Revelation 14:15, the angel tells Jesus Christ to take his sickle and reap the harvest, for he says that the harvest of the earth is ripe. Read on in Revelation 14:16. It says that the earth was harvested. When I read this, this sounds like another description of the rapture that happened in Revelation 7:9-10.

When you read Matthew 24:30-31 (NIV), you will read a description of the rapture that sounds very similar to Revelation 14:16. That passage in Matthew says, *"At that time the sign of the Son of Man will appear in the sky and all the nations of the earth will mourn. They will see the Son of Man coming on the clouds of the sky, with power and great glory. And he will send his angels with a loud trumpet call, and they will gather his elect from the four winds, from one end of the heavens to the other."* When you continue to read Rev. 14:17-19, it talks about a second harvest of the earth, harvested and thrown into the winepress of God's wrath. When you go back to the time of the rapture as described in Revelation 7, you will see that the wrath of God starts in Revelation, chapters 8 and 9. When I first discovered this, I figured that Revelation 7 and 14 were like two places in Revelation that covered the same event, basically showing not all of Revelation is in chronological order. This thought made sense to me until I pondered further and eventually got stumped as I studied the 144,000 mentioned in Revelation 14.

As I was reading Revelation 14:3 (NIV): *"And they sang a new song before the throne"*, *this* really confused me, for this was showing that the 144,000 were with Christ around the throne, <u>before</u> the rapture described in Revelation 14:14. This really did not seem possible that these Jews would be with Christ around the throne before the rapture; because, this would contradict Revelation 9:4!

This passage describes the fifth trumpet of God's wrath, where the scorpion-like locusts are instructed not to harm the grass or trees but only those who did not have the mark of God on their foreheads. This verse shows the 144,000 Jews as being on the earth during the wrath of God, but they are not being harmed by God's wrath. So, you see why I was confused to see these Jews at the throne before the rapture as described in Revelation 14:14.

I asked God in prayer to please show me why this seemed so confusing. I started rereading Revelation chapters 7-14, several times. On the third reading, it was like a light bulb came on, and I saw two separate verses that opened these chapters to a much clearer understanding. In fact, I was so excited; I could hardly contain it.

If you go back and read about the seven seals that start in Revelation 6, you will notice an interlude between the sixth and seventh seals. This interlude in chapter 7 is where the 144,000 are sealed, and then the rapture is described. Next, when you read Revelation 8, the seventh seal is opened, and the seven trumpets of God's wrath start to sound.

These continue through the sixth trumpet of God's wrath at the end of Revelation 9. Then there is another interruption just before the sounding of the seventh trumpet of God's wrath. During this interruption it describes a few different events in Revelation 10 and the first half of Revelation 11. It is in this section I saw the first key to understanding why I was confused with the second description of the 144,000 Jews in Revelation 14.

If you read Revelation 10, you will see that during this interruption, it is describing a second, smaller scroll that is opened and read by John the Revelator. After John read the scroll, he was told in Revelation 10:11 (NIV): *"Then I was told, 'You must prophesy again about many peoples, nations, languages, and kings."* What is happening here is, John, the writer of Revelation, is being told to prophesy again about the people who suddenly appear around the throne in Revelation 7:9. These are the same ones who, I believe, were the raptured and martyred saints which the elder was asking about in Revelation 7. So from Revelation 10:11 until the second description of the rapture, that is referred to as harvest of the earth in Revelation 14:9, John is given further insights into a number of events.

These chapters, Revelation 10:11-14:2 contain some events that are pre-rapture events and show that this section of Revelation is not chronologically in order. Shortly, I will go into more detail about some of the events mentioned here. You will see some exciting events that will take place before the rapture, as described in both Revelation chapter 7 and 14.

First, I want to show you how I saw there is no contradiction concerning the 144,000 Jews who were described as being around the throne with Jesus in Revelation 14. If you will read Revelation 14:1(NIV) it says, *"Then I looked and there before me was the Lamb, standing on Mount Zion and*

24

with him 144,000 who had his name and his Father's name written on their foreheads." The key is that the Lamb is standing on Mount Zion. This event does not take place until Jesus returns to the earth at the end of the Great Tribulation. These verses just show that some of these events in Revelation 10:11 through Revelation 14 are not in chronological order.

While meditating on these verses describing the 144,000, I noticed a verse that posed another dilemma. Revelation 14:4 (NIV): says, *"They were purchased from among men and offered as first-fruits to God and the Lamb."* The problem I noticed in this verse was that they are described as being offered to God and the Lamb as first-fruits. This term, first-fruits, is often seen as a reference to the first-fruits of the resurrection. How can the 144,000 Jews sealed in Revelation 7 be the first-fruits of the resurrection when the saints are raptured before these Jews get resurrected bodies at the end of the Great Tribulation? One logical explanation I see is when the 144,000 are sealed to do God's mission on the earth throughout the time of God's wrath, they could be given their resurrected bodies. When they are sealed and receive resurrected bodies in Revelation chapter 7, they would be the first-fruits of the resurrection <u>before</u> the rapture of the saints takes place in Revelation 7:9. This explanation answers a lot of questions about the 144,000 Jews who are chosen to do a special mission for God.

When you read Revelation 9:4, about how the scorpion locusts are unable to harm the 144,000, it would make sense they could not be harmed if they have resurrected bodies. Many teachers say the mission of these Jews is to be evangelists to the Jews around the world and to point the Jews to Jesus as the Messiah who first came 2,000 years ago. The Jews did not recognize Christ the first time. Think about this, these 144,000 Jews appear on the scene just before the rapture as described in Revelation 7:9. This is the time when the antichrist is waging war against the saints; then when the two witnesses appear, the antichrist wages war against them. But nowhere does it say that satan or the antichrist is waging war against the 144,000 chosen Jews. If they were given their resurrected bodies at the time that they are sealed, then satan could not touch them, as they are no longer living in a mortal body. A further thought that reinforces this explanation is, if you look at the daunting task these sealed Jews have, they have to go throughout the world during this time when the antichrist will have them marked as terrorists. It will not be easy for them to travel freely, let alone be able to make it through airport security with a mark on their foreheads, telling everyone that I am a special emissary sent from God.

If they have been given their resurrected bodies, they will be able to get their assignments supernaturally from God and will be able to travel supernaturally as Christ did when he came back to the earth with his resurrected body. This allowed Jesus to appear and disappear or walk through walls. So, if the 144,000 specially chosen Jews will be able to move freely and instantly to whatever destination God sends them without any fear of harm from the antichrist or man, they will accomplish God's will to reach the Jews scattered throughout the world in record time.

Now think about this, if it makes sense that the 144,000 Jews are sealed and given resurrected bodies in Revelation 7 and they are the first-fruits of the Resurrection, then how can the rapture of the church be Revelation 4:1? The saints and the 144,000 Jews cannot both be the first-fruits. **Also think about this, first fruits denotes a small portion of the harvest. It makes more sence that the 144,000 are first fruits (a portion of the harvest) than the harvest of the saints that cannot be numbered. Also realize the**

26

144,000 cannot be first fruits if the rapture happened in Revelation 4:1.

I said earlier I would cover some of the events contained in these chapters in Revelation, that John the Revelator was instructed to prophesy again, concerning the peoples to be raptured. I believe the section that contains these events is from the beginning of Revelation 11 to the second description of the rapture in Revelation 14:14. This section is out of chronological order. Some of these events covered here go back before the rapture, and some events go forward to when Christ physically returns to the earth and stands on Mt. Zion. Some events are in between.

The first event I believe John was prophesying about that would have a connection to the people to be raptured concerns the two witnesses. The two witnesses are on the earth for three and one-half years. If they are killed by the antichrist before the end of the seven years of the Great Tribulation, then this means that they appear at some point before the middle of the seven years. This makes it possible, if the rapture happens at some point close to the middle of the seven years, for the saints to witness the appearing of the two witnesses before the rapture. To me, this is very exciting, for this will be another supernatural event God will send to the earth to show those who are lost that Jesus is coming soon and wants to attract as many as possible to himself before the rapture. As I study Revelation 12 and 13, there is so much to grasp for each piece of the prophetic puzzle to fit together. I believe some of the prophecies here will not be fully understood until future events begin to unfold.

In conclusion of this section of my study, I would like to point out an event I believe we will witness before the rapture. This portion of my study is found in Revelation 14 before it talks about the harvest of the earth mentioned in

Revelation 14:14, which I believe is a second description of the rapture. Revelation 14:6-11 covers the coming of three angels sent by God to bring a message to the world. If you go back and read Revelation 7:1-2, you will read about four angels on the earth. Then it says in Revelation 7:2, (NIV): *"Then I saw another angel coming up from the east, having the seal of the living God..."* This angel goes on to call the other four angels to help him put the seal of the living God on the 144,000 Jews. Read Revelation 7:3, (NIV): *"Do not harm the land or the sea or the trees until WE put the seal on the foreheads of the servants of our God."*

If you will read this portion carefully, you realize these angels who are asked to help seal the 144,000 Jews are the ones who will deliver the wrath of God, but they have been asked to hold off until some point after the sealing of the 144,000 Jews. **This is another key Scripture pointing out the wrath of God does not start until some point after the sealing of the 144,000.**

An interesting observation is, there will be many angels involved during this seven-year period. When you go to Revelation 14:6 (NIV), the same phrase is used: *"Then I saw another angel flying in midair..."* As you read this, you will discover that this angel has a mission to those living on the earth. Read Revelation 14:6-7, (NIV*): "Then I saw another angel flying in midair, and he had the eternal gospel to proclaim to those who live on the earth - to every nation, tribe, language, and people. He said in a loud voice. 'Fear God and give him glory, because the hour of his judgment has come. Worship him who made the heavens, the earth, the sea and the springs of water."* It is so exciting that this angel is sent to proclaim the gospel to those who live on the earth.

Going into detail, he describes the people he is speaking to in the same terms as those who will be involved in the rapture later in Revelation 14:6-7 as the people from every nation, tribe, language, and people. He is speaking again of the Gentiles who are eligible for the rapture. As you read further, he proclaims what man is to do before the judgment of God starts, for it says, *"Fear God and give him glory, because the hour of his judgment has come."* This verse is important to understand.

What I have been showing is, these chapters are not in chronological order. As you see, it says the hour of his judgment has come. But when you read Revelation 8 and 9, the judgment or the wrath of God starts after what I see as the rapture in chapter 7. This is illustrated with the warning from the first of three angels, for the nations to repent before the wrath of God to comes, as described in the second description of the rapture in Revelation 14.

Therefore, the first angel is given the mission of helping the saints to bring in the last part of the harvest before the rapture happens and the wrath of God begins. **There are not two raptures but rather two accounts describing the same event with God's wrath following.**

Next, Revelation 14:8 goes on to talk about the second angel: *"A second angel followed and said, 'Fallen! Fallen is Babylon the Great, which made all nations drink the maddening wine of her adulteries."* I believe that Babylon the Great that will fall is America. I go into this in greater detail later in this study. I believe when it says Babylon the Great has fallen, it is referring to governmental, social, and economic collapse, not the full destruction of Babylon that is to come later as described in Revelation 18.

I believe this collapse could be triggered by a few possible events. One possible choice would be that we would be taken out by our enemies. Another could be the catastrophic event described in the sixth seal of Revelation. I go into this event in greater detail later in my chapter called "The window of the Lord's return". This event would bring America to a new low.

Next, Revelation 14:9 talks about the third angel following the first two, and the wording conveys that the three angels will appear in chronological order. The third angel is proclaiming the judgment of God and the eternal punishment about to come on those who fail to heed this message. At a time when the church will be under great persecution and will have moved underground to avoid the oppression of the antichrist, these angels will move about openly proclaiming the Gospel. This will take away any excuse that man would have about knowing God's plan of redemption.

As you read these verses in Revelation 14:9-12, you will see that the mark of the beast is being forced on the world at this time. Christians and all who do not want to come under God's judgment must at all costs refuse this mark and the system of the antichrist. Remember, the wording of the three angels show this is chronological; verse 12 is a message to the saints. It is telling the saints that this will be a trying time, but we must remain faithful to Jesus, as the rewards are great.

This next verse confirms there will be trying times, and we must be faithful at all costs. Hebrews 10:35-38 (NIV) states, *"So do not throw away your confidence; it will be richly rewarded. You need to persevere so that when you have done the will of God, you will receive what he has promised. For in just a little while, he who is coming will come and will not delay. But my righteous ones will live by faith. And if he shrinks back, I will not be pleased with him."* Read; Revelation 14:9-12, (NIV): *"A third angel followed them and said in a loud voice: 'If anyone worships the beast and his image and receives his mark on the forehead or on the hand, he too, will drink of the wine of the wrath of God's fury, which has been poured full strength* *into the cup of his wrath. He will be tormented with burning sulfur in the presence of the holy angels and of the Lamb. And the smoke of their torment rises forever and ever. **There is no rest day or night for those who worship the beast and his image, or for anyone who receives the mark of his name.** This calls for the patient endurance on the part of the saints who obey God's commandments and remain faithful to Jesus."* As we approach the coming of the Lord, we will be facing challenging times. Many Christians are fearful they will have to go through any part of the Great Tribulation. Some Christians convey the thought that how could a loving God allow his people to go through any of this tribulation?

I believe we must have the same resolve to serve God as the saints of the early church had. They were not just willing to live for God; they were willing to die for God. This was not as a way of obtaining grace and salvation. It was because they already had God's grace and salvation. Look at what happened to the disciples who were first imprisoned and then released by an angel. When they were brought before the religious leaders who wanted to kill them, listen to the attitude of these early believers that were under trials and persecution. Read Acts 5:40-41 (NIV): *"...They called the apostles in and had them flogged. Then they ordered them not to speak in the name of Jesus and let them go. The apostles left the Sanhedrin, rejoicing, because they had been counted worthy of suffering disgrace for the Name."*

Look at what happened in China when Mao took over, he had thousands of Christians killed. The 80,000 Christians in China had to go underground, but did they give up their faith? No! The church oppressed with tribulation and persecution in China grew from 80,000 to a somewhere between 100 - 200 million Christians today. We are God's army and we must recognize that as we get closer to the

Lord's return, that satan will be ramping up his attack on the earth to keep people from getting saved.

It just does not make sense that God would take the saints out before the harvest is complete. Read 2 Peter 3:9 (NIV): *"The Lord is not slow in keeping his promise, as some understand slowness. He is patient with you, not wanting anyone to perish, but everyone to come to repentence."*

If God is so determined to bring the lost to himself that he would send angels to help in the last days before his return, does it not make sense that God would leave his army here to lead the lost to Christ until the last minute and THEN rapture his saints off the earth just before he pours out his wrath and judgment on those who have rejected him?

3. How does the United States fit into the prophetic picture?

This is a question that has intrigued me forever. The Bible does not address the United States in plain-speak, so you have to wonder how do we fit into all this? I guess an easy answer would be that we just become absorbed into and under the rule of the antichrist. Our Constitution is cancelled, and the USA becomes irrelevant as we know it. **I was told by one pastor that it might be that the United States will be left out of the events concerning the antichrist and the mark of the beast altogether. Do not hold your breath on that hope. That is truly wishful thinking. Do you really think that satan, indwelling a world leader who has designs to rule the planet forever, would think of leaving America to be free to do its own thing? To fully dispel this thought, read Revelation 13:7 (NIV):** *"He was given power to make war against the saints and to conquer them. And he was given authority over EVERY tribe, people, language, and NATION."* **America is a nation.**

Over the years, my thoughts on this subject have led me to see that we have been the main protector of Israel, thus causing the United States to be standing in the way of many of the prophetic events that have to fall into place. As long as the United States is a strong superpower, we would not stand by and let Israel be attacked and destroyed, as we have always provided them with armaments and supplies. This simple belief has brought me to some interesting thoughts over the years. The early thoughts I had were as follows:

1) We would be defeated in a world war, and we would not be around to do any more protecting.

2) The United States would have an economic collapse which would make us so poor that we could no longer hold the position as Israel's protector and as the world cop. Also, our problems would be so severe at home that we would need all our military and police forces to keep things under control at home, thus making it so we would not have the resources to deal with world problems anymore. This is difficult to envision, I do not want to see these kinds of hard times. I certainly do not want to experience an event like the Great Depression of the thirties that hit my father's generation, but I have always believed that for the end-time events to unfold, according to that which has been laid out in the Bible, then America and the world would have to experience a widespread economic collapse.

3) My next thought is a long one and the most thought provoking. I have questioned the Scriptures I am about to share with you, wondering for years if these Scriptures could be talking about the United States. If it were not for the fact that I have read other prophetic writer's sharing my questions and possible conclusions, I would hesitate to share these thoughts.

Where do we begin? If you read Revelation 18, about the destruction of Mystery Babylon, you have to wonder if America could be a spiritual or a type of the actual, real physical, geographically located Babylon. Most Bible teachers believe these Scriptures are talking about Iraq. But when you carefully read the passage, you will see many Scriptures that show the country of Iraq does not fit the description of the country to be destroyed in judgment.

Here is an example: Revelation 18:10 (NIV): says, *"Woe! Woe! O great city, O Babylon, city of power! In one hour your doom has come!"* **Iraq is not a city of power today;** they had their day, and so the question I have is whether

How does the United States fit into the prophetic picture?

these Scriptures are talking about a country that has the spirit of Babylon and not the geographic Iraq of today. If you read these Scriptures with that thought in mind and apply the thought that the city of power it is talking about is the United States, then see if it makes sense to you.

For example read, Revelation 17:1-2 (NIV): *"...Come, I will show you the punishment of the great prostitute, who sits on many waters. With her the kings of the earth committed adultery and the inhabitants of the earth were intoxicated with the wine of her adulteries."* Geographically, the USA sits on many waters and contains many peoples from many nationalities, and Iraq does not. Now read, Revelation 17:15 (NIV): *"The waters you saw, where the prostitute sits are peoples, multitudes, nations and languages."* America is a land known as a land of many peoples and languages, and Iraq is not. Revelation 17:18 (NIV) says, *"The woman you saw is the great city that rules over the kings of the earth."* This sounds like the USA, not Iraq.

Revelation 18:1-3 talks about the fall of this great city and Revelation 18:4 (NIV) says, *"Come out of her my people"* I have been doing a bit of a study on this verse, focusing on the two words "my people"; because, at first I thought it referred to Christians. Now I see the strong possibility it is addressing the Jews as God's chosen people. In 2 Chronicles 7:14, it says, *"If my people who are called by my name will humble themselves and pray and seek my face and turn from their wicked ways, then will I hear from heaven and will forgive their sin and heal their land."* This verse is God speaking to his people, the Jews, in answer to their prayers when they were praying to God during the dedication of the temple. This phrase, "my people", is most often used to refer to God's chosen people, the Jews. If you look at Romans 9:25, you will see it can also mean the Gentiles who have been accepted as God's people because of Christ's sacrifice on the cross. Romans 9:25 (NIV): *"...I will call them my people' who are not my people; and I will call her my loved one' who is not my loved one."* When you study Revelation, you will see the Christians are spoken about collectively as the church or referred to as saints. It is my conclusion the reference to "my people" in Revelation 18:4 is speaking to the Jews after the rapture has taken place. I will go into greater detail in the next chapter entitled, "God's no man left behind".

As we continue to look at the possibility that Mystery Babylon is going to be destroyed, it can seem a bit unnerving and depressing. I have to point out that if we are talking about the total destruction of America, we can rejoice that before its destruction, God will evacuate his people before he lets loose his wrath of destruction. Read, Revelation 18:17-18 (NIV): *"In one hour, such great wealth has been brought to ruin! Every sea captain, and all who travel by ship, the sailors and all who earn their living from the sea, will stand far off, when they see the smoke of her burning, they will exclaim, 'Was there ever a city like this great city?"* Does this sound like Iraq or the USA? Also, ask yourself, "What other country could this chapter be talking about?" Well, any Bible scholar would eliminate Russia and China. It would not be Europe, as this is the center of the antichrist's rule, and the revived Roman Empire is the country that is ready to destroy mystery Babylon. Some say mystery Babylon is Rome, ruled by the Pope. I do not see this as a land of commerce over which the merchants of the world would mourn. Could it be a Middle Eastern country like Iraq? I would have to say no for two reasons. First, the description of this country just does not fit any of the countries of the Middle East, and the Bible says the antichrist wants to ultimately destroy Israel. If the Middle Eastern countries want Israel destroyed, then this makes these countries friends of the antichrist. I am sorry; I just do not

36

How does the United States fit into the prophetic picture?

see any choice but to say this is describing the fall of the United States. This country is described as mystery Babylon. Think about this; the United States is the only superpower today that did not exist when the Bible was written. If the country that is being described did exist during the writing of Revelation, then would it be a mystery?

If you were to ask, "Does the Bible really tell us who God would use to destroy the country we are talking about?" The answer lies in Revelation 17:16 (NIV): *"The beast and the ten horns you saw will hate the prostitute. They will bring her to ruin, and leave her naked; they will eat her flesh and burn her with fire."*

Now after hearing about the fall of the dollar, the rise of the euro, and the new European leader, it gets easier to see what this verse in Revelation is talking about. I believe this is America, based on my discussion above about the fall of Babylon spoken about in Revelation 18. The leaders behind the new revived Roman Empire and the antichrist will not want to see the US dollar rise again and certainly will not want to see the USA rise to world power again.

I believe one possible scenario is the great numbers of Muslims in Europe will make a pact with the revived Roman Empire to stop backing Israel, and the USA will be left hanging out there all alone. An update now shows us that the United States, under the leadership of those who do not support Israel, will pull back our support and ultimately let Israel stand on its own without any outside help.

In concluding this chapter, let it be fully realized, that Israel will never be left alone without protection. When it looks like Israel is without allies, the armies of God will be encamped around Israel, and Israel will never be destroyed.

4. God's "No Man Left Behind"

If this study has given you some second thoughts, as it has me, that the rapture does not happen until Revelation 7, then maybe, you will also be convinced, as I am, that we will not see the rapture until after the sealing of the 144,000 Jews. This is explained in Revelation 7:3-8. Now read Revelation 7:9 (NIV): *"After this, I looked and there before me was a great multitude that no one could count, from every nation, tribe, and   people and language, standing before the throne and in front of the Lamb. They were wearing white robes and were holding palm branches in their hands."* I believe this is the rapture as seen from the throne in heaven. After we meet the Lord in the clouds, our Savior will lead us to his home and throne where we will worship God and our Lord and Savior Jesus Christ.

Next, read Revelation 7:10 (KJV), where you will see the raptured saints having a great time of worship and praise: *"And cried with a loud voice, saying, salvation to our God which sitteth upon the throne, and unto the Lamb."* Now if you read Revelation 7:13-14, you will see the rapture event happening so fast that one of the elders constantly around the throne of God appeared to have missed the event and asks a question of surprise. *"Where did this multitude that no one could number, come from?"* Revelation 7:13-14 (KJV): says, *"Who are these which are arrayed in white robes? And whence came they?"* And I said unto him, 'Sir, thou knowest.' And he said to me, *"These are they which came out of the Great Tribulation, and have washed their robes, and made them white in the blood of the Lamb."* The next three verses of Revelation 7:15-17, totally supports what will happen to the saints when they arrive in heaven. Read Revelation 7:15-17 (NIV): *"Therefore, they are before the throne of God and*

*serve him day and night in his temple; and he who sits on
the throne will spread his tent over them. Never again will
they hunger; never again will they thirst. The sun will not
beat upon them, nor any scorching heat. For the Lamb at
the center of the throne will be their Shepherd; he will lead
them to springs of living water. And God will wipe away
every tear from their eyes."*

Next, go to Revelation 8 where you will read about the
seven angels who hold the seven trumpets of God's wrath
that is about to rain on the earth. You realize how God
manifests his grace to his saints by rescuing them from the
earth just before the out-pouring of his wrath.

Going back to the sealing of the 144,000 Jews, there is an
important sequence in this event. These Jews are sealed in
Revelation 7:1-8. Then at some point after the sealing, you
have the rapture of the saints taking place. Think about this;
it is perfect timing. When Christ was on the earth and his
people, the children of Israel, rejected him as a nation, he
promised to graft the Jews who rejected him back into his
family. I believe a step further is to realize that they are to
be an important part of the bride of Christ.

In Revelation 7, we see the turning-point at which time
God is getting ready to move his saints out of harm's way
through the rapture, and he turns his attention to bringing
the nation of Israel back into his family. He has just commissioned the 144,000 Jewish evangelists to preach Christ
to the Jews throughout the world. Now you might wonder
how God could pour out his wrath on the earth while his
chosen people Israel are still on the earth. After further
study, I believe once God seals the 144,000, there will be
only a short time before the rapture. During that short time,
the 144,000 Jewish evangelists will launch the greatest
evangelistic blitz of all time to let Jews around the world
know Jesus is their coming Messiah, and he is coming

imminently to take them to his heavenly Father and introduce them as an important part of his bride.

I believe that when the rapture occurs many Jews will go up at this time. Those who are left behind, God will still extend his hand of protection to. I want to show you how I believe God will protect his people, the Jews who are left behind. The Bible teaches that the plagues cannot hurt the 144,000 sealed Jews. Read Revelation 9:1-6 (NIV): *"The fifth angel sounded his trumpet, and I saw a star that had fallen from the sky to the earth. The star was given the key to the shaft of the Abyss. When he opened the Abyss, smoke rose from it like the smoke from a gigantic furnace. The sun and sky were darkened by the smoke from the Abyss. And out of the smoke locusts came down upon the earth and were given power like that of scorpions of the earth. They were told not to harm the grass of the earth or any plant or tree, but only those people who did not have the seal of God on their foreheads. They were not given power to kill them, but only to torture them for five months. And the agony they suffered was like that of the sting of a scorpion when it strikes a man. During those days men will seek death, but will not find it; they will long to die, but death will elude them."*

When the rapture occurs, those Jews who have just accepted Christ in this massive evangelistic effort will go up in the rapture along with all the Christian Gentiles, (including the dead in Christ, and those Christians who are alive at that time.) Recently, I believe God gave me further insight on a verse that previously confused me, Matthew 24:30-31, (NIV*): "At that time the sign of the Son of Man will appear in the sky, and the nations of the earth will mourn. They will see the Son of Man coming on the clouds of the sky, with power and great glory. And he will send his angels with a loud trumpet call and they will gather his elect from the four winds, from one end of the heavens to the other."*

40

I used to be confused as to why the nations of the earth would mourn at the time of the rapture; because, those left behind will have accepted the antichrist as their god and curse God. I believe once someone takes the mark of the beast, they no longer have a heart capable of repenting.

In the King James version, it uses the term 'tribes' instead of 'nations'. I believe this verse is speaking of the tribes of Israel in all the nations of the world. I believe when the 144,000 Jewish evangelists reach out to every Jew on earth, many will recognize Jesus is really their Messiah and Savior, and will go up in the rapture. Those Jews who still reject this message will be allowed to witness Christ's coming in the clouds at the time of the rapture. Those Jews will realize that they have just rejected Christ Jesus as their Messiah for the second time. The first time was at the time of Christ's crucifixion and then again at his second coming for his bride. The Jews from all nations around the world will mourn when they realize what they have done.

If you will read the book of Zechariah, you will see at the time of the Second Coming and the battle of Armageddon, the Jews have their eyes opened and cry in repentance for rejecting Christ as their messiah. Zechariah 12:10-11 (NIV): *"And I will pour out on the house of David and the inhabitants of Jerusalem a spirit of grace and supplication. They will look on me, the one they have pierced, and they will mourn for him as one mourns for an only child, and grieve bitterly for him as one grieves for a firstborn son. On that day the weeping in Jerusalem will be great, like the weeping of Hadad Rimmon in the plain of Megiddo."*

Now let us return again to the subject of God's providing for his 144,000 special servants after the rapture. They cannot be touched. When you carefully read Revelation 9:4, you understand it specifically points out only God's

144,000 sealed with his mark will be spared from this tormenting plague. This brings up two very important questions. The first is," If there were Tribulation saints, as many prophetic scholars believe, where is the provision for their protection from these plagues?" I consider this further reason to believe there are no Tribulation saints after the rapture. The second question is, "What will happen to God's chosen people Israel during this time?" I will show you how I believe God has made provision to protect his chosen people during this time.

Let us go back to the 144,000 Jews who have been sealed and commissioned to take the Gospel of Christ to the nation of Israel. I believe part of their commission is to warn the Jews that Jesus is their Messiah and he is coming for those who accepted him. After this, the plagues of God's wrath will fall on the earth. I believe I can show you from God's Word that the children of Israel who miss the rapture will be told to leave all nations where they are living and head back to the Holy Land before the plagues start to fall.

Remember when Moses told his people in Egypt to get ready for the Passover by sacrificing a lamb to cover and protect their home and families from the angel of death? The 144,000 sealed Jews have this same kind of protection from the plagues that are about to come upon the earth. Remember when God was sending plagues like the locusts that ate all the crops of the Egyptians? If you read carefully about this account in the Old Testament, you will notice in the land of Goshen, the children of Israel were protected. The plagues did not harm the land of God's people. I believe it is possible to show from Scripture that God is going to call his people home to Israel just before his plagues and wrath fall upon man and the earth.

This is a good time to read Revelation 18, which talks about the fall of Mystery Babylon. I have already said that I believe that Mystery Babylon is the USA, which happens to be the home of millions of Jews. Before the destruction of Mystery Babylon, the Jews will be warned to leave before destruction hits. Remember, God's wrath and plagues start to fall in Revelation 8 <u>following</u> the rapture. The saints in the USA and around the world have already left in the rapture. The Jews who have not accepted Christ as their Messiah will be left behind at the time of the rapture, but God will still make provision for them to escape his soon coming wrath.

Read Revelation 18:4 (NIV): *"And I heard another voice from heaven say, 'Come out of her, my people, that ye be not partakers of her sins, and that ye receive not of her plagues."* I used to think that this was either a rapture verse or a command for Christians to leave the USA before God's wrath fell. There are two problems with this thinking. If this were a verse about the rapture, God would not have to ask us to leave. We would just go instantly. If it were to mean the Christians are to leave the USA physically, then where would millions of Christians go? Would Canada or Mexico open its borders for all of these Christians? I do not think so.

Another writer on the end-times wrote an interesting explanation in his book on the last days. He said he believes the text in Revelation that says "Come out of her, my people" is speaking to American Christians to leave the USA and take flight to Israel for protection. I see a real problem with this interpretation. Do you believe that Israel will open its doors for millions of American Christians to come to Israel to wait for the Lord's return? I do not think so.

The only thing that makes sense to me is that God will instruct the Jews who missed the rapture, after being warned by the 144,000 sealed Jewish evangelists, to head for cover, to leave Mystery Babylon and the other nations of the earth

43

and to return to their homeland. Now think about this, if it were gentile Christians trying to flee the USA, would Israel open its doors? I do not think so. However, Israel has always had its doors open for the Jews to return to their own nation Israel. I believe once these Jews flee to Israel, God will supernaturally protect them from harm just as he did the Jews in Egypt during the time of Moses.

A Scripture verse that goes well with what I am sharing here is found in Ezekiel 39:27-28 (NIV): *"When I have brought them back from the nations and have gathered them from the countries of their enemies, I will show myself holy through them in the sight of many nations. Then they will know that I am the LORD, their God, for though I sent them into exile among the nations, I will gather them to their own land, not leaving any behind. I will no longer hide my face from them, for I will pour out my Spirit on the house of Israel, declares the Sovereign LORD."*

I covered more about the 144,000 in an earlier chapter where I portrayed how I believe these specially chosen Jews will be able to accomplish their mission for God with supernatural, resurrected bodies. The two witnesses will also have super-natural powers but will have mortal bodies, for the Bible clearly states that they will be killed and lay in the streets of Jerusalem for three and one half days before being resurrected for the whole world to see, (Revelation 11:7-13). These two witnesses will also be on the earth at the time when the Jews are being evacuated to Israel.

5. Can Gentiles be saved after the rapture?

Over the years, I have heard a few scenarios concerning this question. Some may ask, "But who are the Gentiles?" They are anyone from any nation or people group who are not Jewish.

1. One scenario is there will be Tribulation saints who knew about God's plan of Salvation but did not accept Christ or live for him before the rapture. They would turn to Christ during the Great Tribulation and not accept the mark of the beast. They would struggle through the Great Tribulation and become the Tribulation saints. This explanation is necessary in order to have a pre-Tribulation rapture theory. If the rapture does not happen until Revelation 7, then the term "Tribulation saints" would not be necessary, for all the saints would be raptured at the same time. Further evidence of this scenario is the fact there is no mention of saints on the earth during the outpouring of God's wrath. Also, God makes provision for the wrath of God not to hurt the 144,000 but makes no provision for Tribulation saints! The best example is the scorpion creatures that could not hurt the 144,000 sealed with God's mark. Why is there no provision for the saints to be protected from these creatures of God's wrath? The best explanation is all the saints are raptured before this time of God's wrath on the earth.

2. Here is another scenario. The Holy Spirit would be removed during the Great Tribulation. The basis of this statement comes from the teaching that the saints are raptured off the earth and have the Holy Spirit living in them. When this happens, the Holy Spirit's influence will be taken off the earth with them. The question this generates in my mind is, if the Holy Spirit is not working to draw sinners to Christ, how will people be saved during this time? Some might say if you cannot accept and serve God with the Holy Spirit's help, how can you do it without the Holy Spirit's help? Yet as I see it, the Holy Spirit is God, who is omnipresent, and you cannot remove God from the earth.

3. My father-in-law, the Rev. Edgar Rasmussen, has always maintained that to tell people they can be saved after the rapture is a shaky position at best. It gives people a false hope of a second chance. Holding out a second chance does not draw the unsaved and the backsliders to Christ. It tells them they can stay in their unsaved condition and still have a way back to God after the rapture occurs.

There are many who believe the saints have to be raptured before the Great Tribulation; because, the Bible says, "he that restraineth, must be taken out of the way before the antichrist can be revealed." I believe this view has too many contradictions in God's word. Basically, this view says the rapture has to come before the antichrist can be revealed; therefore, the rapture is a pre-Tribulation event. But this interpretation contradicts, 2 Thessalonians 2:3 (NIV): *"Don't let anyone deceive you in any way, for that day will not come until the rebellion occurs and the man of lawlessness is revealed, the man doomed to destruction."* I do not believe the restrainer is the Holy Spirit and I will offer a compelling argument for who the restrainer is later in chapter 8.

My position on this question has been becoming clearer while doing this study on the end-times. If you take the position that there is a pre-Tribulation rapture, then you have to assume the saints mentioned during the opening of the seals in Revelation 6 are tribulation saints. This is traditional thinking. As I have pointed out, if the rapture does not happen until after the opening of the sixth seal in Revelation 6, actually happening in Revelation 7:9-13, then a very interesting observation can be made. Before I make this observation, I should point out that you can see the rapture event along with other important events happening in two sections of Revelation. You will see the 144,000 Jews and the rapture following in both Revelation 7 and 14. You need to read these chapters together to get the whole picture, just as you would read the first four books of the New Testament to see the whole story of the Gospel.

This brings me to that very interesting observation I mentioned above and possibly the answer to the question, "Can Gentiles be saved after the rapture?" If you look at Revelation 7 and 14, which contain the same rapture event, and continue reading on to the coming of Christ at the end of the Great Tribulation, you will see no living saints mentioned after the rapture. Think about this; if the church has to go through the first half of the Great Tribulation, many exciting things will happen. Those who have fallen away will come back to Christ. The church will wake up and get the message of salvation out like never before in history, and as the day of the Gentiles is coming to a close after the sealing of the 144,000 Jews, every wise Christian will realize, as I have mentioned, we are in the final countdown of days on this side of eternity. Our 401k's will not do us any good, and only what is done for Christ will last. I believe that during this time, super evangelism will be taking place, and all who will come to Christ will come.

During this time, the church will see a time of spiritual warfare unlike anything the world has ever seen. All will have to make a decision to either accept what Christ has to offer, eternal life with tribulation for a little while, or accept the comfort and benefits of what the antichrist has to offer, a full belly. Hmmmm, is this not what Esau took for his birthright? The point is there will be no need for anymore decisions to accept Christ after the rapture. The time will be over for making decisions. I realize there will be exceptions to this; I believe there will be some people living in remote areas of the earth that will be outside of the influence of the antichrist, and if they survive the last years of the Great Tribulation, they will be included among those who will repopulate the earth during the millennium.

In closing, think of this. If the rapture is pre-Tribulation, the church stays in its lukewarm condition, waiting around for the rapture while millions of people get left behind. On the other hand, with a mid-Tribulation rapture happening after the opening of the seals during the first half of the Great Tribulation, then what happens is exciting. The church will wake up to what is about to take place. We will see the greatest revival in the history of the church. I believe we will also see a great falling away at the same time. When the church realizes what they were told about a pre-Tribulation rapture was in error, many Christians will become bitter towards God, and feel God has abandoned them, and they will give in to the New World system.

Even though this scenario is scary, look at the positive things that would happen. The church ushers in the greatest revival the world has ever seen, and the saints are purified into the pure bride for which, the Bible says, Christ is coming back. This makes so much sense to me. Going through the fire of the Great Tribulation will purify and grow the Bride of Christ. The Bible says in 2Peter 3:9b, (NIV): *"He is patient with you, not wanting anyone to perish, but everyone to come to repentance."*

If I had my choice, the pre-Tribulation rapture would be a far more desirable option. Even though the mid-Tribulation scenario is a scary option, it means that millions more of the lost will come to Christ. Remember, many of those millions who have not accepted Christ are your friends and relatives! They are the ones for whom Christ died.

6. Other Bible teachers' perspectives concerning the rapture

After putting many of my thoughts on paper, I started looking on the internet and at available books to see what other Bible teachers were saying; it is interesting what I found. I will be changing the names of the prophetic teachers I use as it is not my purpose to criticize but to search for the truth. I will start this chapter with a study of the Scriptures used by a respected teacher, who I will call Rev. John B. Doe, who teaches the pre-Tribulation rapture view. I will be reviewing the Bible verses he uses to establish his position. I would encourage you to study these verses used by Rev. John B. Doe. I have used some of his verses as a springboard to show why I now believe the Bible teaches the church must be spiritually prepared for the possibility of going through the early years of the Great Tribulation.

I have done a similar study looking at the teachings of other prophetic teachers, who I will call Philip Doe and David Doe. These men are great teachers but I believe many great teachers are defending a position to the point of possible spiritual blindness, a position handed down from their fathers and other generations before them.

I am not Paul, but what he wrote in the book of Acts is a worthwhile challenge to all of us, specifically in Acts 17:11 (NIV): *"Now the Bereans were of more noble character then the Thessalonians, for they received the message with great eagerness and examined the Scriptures every day to see if what Paul said was true."*

John B. Doe

49

John B. Doe, has had a great ministry of teaching the chronology of God's dispensations and prophetic plans. He uses a huge chart he set up on the platforms of churches and auditoriums where he ministers. When I recently studied his small roll-out version of this chart, I noticed that he had about a dozen Bible verses under the topic of the rapture. Based on the placement of these verses on his chart, it is obvious that he believes in a pre-Tribulation rapture. He has placed these verses, on his chart, between the seven churches of Revelation found in Revelation 2 and 3 but before the opening of the seals found in Revelation 6.

It is widely accepted that close to the opening of the seals is the beginning of the seven-year Great Tribulation period. Those who hold to the pre-Tribulation view believe that the rapture will take place before the Great Tribulation gets started. I studied through Rev. John B. Doe's list of verses, looking for ones that would show the timing of the rapture. What I found in these verses was interesting. Basically, these verses attest to the resurrection of the righteous. They also attest to the rapture, but they do not really show Scripturally that the rapture is a pre-Tribulation event. In fact, there is one verse he uses that you could use to say that the rapture is a post-Tribulation event. Interestingly, this verse is the only verse I have found so far that shows the timing of the rapture is different than my conclusion of being a mid-Tribulation event. I will go over this verse in detail when I work my way through the verses on his list.

As I stated in a previous chapter, interpretation of Scripture on any doctrinal issue should be backed up with at least two verses to assure correct interpretation of God's word. If I get confused over one verse because it contradicts my conclusion, I will stick with the interpretation I can back-up with two or more Scriptures. I also believe that as I continue to study God's Word, at some point the truth

50

will come to light, and the verse that seems to contradict will eventually line-up with the rest of the Word of God.

Let us start by looking at the many Bible verses that John B. Doe uses to show the rapture of the church. First, I will list all the verses that he has on his chart under the rapture of the church. Then I will show each verse one at a time, and I will do my best to explain why it is relevant to the rapture. I will be looking to see if these verses show that the rapture will be a pre-Tribulation event.

John B. Doe's Scriptures for pre-Tribulation rapture

These are his chosen verses: Luke 21:34-36, John 14:1-3, 1Corinthians 15:23,51-58, 2Corinthians 5:1-8, Ephesians 5:27, Philippians 3:11, 20-21, Colossians 3:4, 1 Thessalonians 2:19, 3:13, 4:13-17, 5:9-23, and 2 Thessalonians 2:1, 7-8.

Luke 21:34-36 (NIV): *"Be careful, or your hearts will be weighed down with dissipation, drunkenness, and the anxieties of life, and that day will close on you unexpectedly like a trap. For it will come upon all those who live on the earth. Be always on the watch, and pray that you may be able to escape all that is about to happen, and that you may be able to stand before the Son of Man."*

When I read this over, I see it talks about a horrible time coming on the earth. I believe there are two periods it could be talking about. The time of the Great Tribulation is the first that comes to mind, but the Bible teaches there will be time of birth pains before the Great Tribulaion starts that will be so bad that many will think the Great Tribulation has already started. I will cover this period of birth pains in more depth in the next chapter on the coming antichrist. These verses are a warning to Christians, not to be so caught up in this world that you do not recognize the time in which we are living. We need to be sure that we are watching for the Lord's return so that we are not caught unawares. These verses infer that we can see this time coming, and it will not be a surprise to us. I want you to look at a portion of these verses with me. Luke 21:36 (NIV): *"Be always on the watch, and pray that you may be able to escape all that is about to happen."* I believe that John B. Doe uses this verse under the rapture; because, it would be easy to think that to escape what is to come will be the wrath of God that we would escape by being raptured.

I want to remind you that if you are a Christian, you do not have to pray that you will go up in the rapture. The rapture will catch up every Christian and take us off this earth in the twinkling of an eye. I believe the Bible teaches us that Christians will go through some trying times and that our God is more than able to protect us in the midst of tribulation. It will be tribulation that we need to pray we escape, not the wrath of God. It is a given that we will escape God's wrath through the rapture.

Look at Daniel's three friends who had to face the fiery furnace. God helped them escape that trial, and I believe if we make God our all and all by putting our total trust in Him, we will see him miraculously preserve us in the worst of times. Yet the Bible says there will be martyred saints during this time. Remember, we will never face any trial alone, for God's Word says, "I will never leave you nor forsake you." Also, when you look at this verse in light of other Scriptures, such as 2 Thessalonians 2:1-3, you see the rapture may be getting close, but until certain events take place, the rapture will not happen.

2 Thessalonians 2:1-3 (NIV): *"Concerning the coming of our Lord Jesus Christ and our being gathered to him, we ask you brothers, not to become easily unsettled or alarmed by some prophecy, report or letter supposed to have come*

from us, saying that the day of the Lord has already come. Don't let anyone deceive you in any way, for that day will not come, until the rebellion occurs and the man of lawlessness is revealed, the man doomed to destruction."

I know the man doomed to destruction is the antichrist and he is yet to be revealed. For the longest time I did not know what the rebellion was about, but now I realize it is a great falling away that will take place before the Lord returns. This verse is talking about the coming antichrist and the falling away in the same verse. I believe that is because the falling away will happen during the time of the antichrist. It is sad, but the church today is weak, and I believe many Christians are convinced the rapture will take us to heaven before times get tough. If the church suddenly sees the hard times of the Great Tribulation and is not prepared for it, when faced with the choice of whether to buy into the antichrist's system or be denied the ability to buy or sell and face possible starvation, many will make the wrong choice. I believe this will be the time of a great falling away. As I have warned previously, Esau sold his birthright for food, so according to God's Word, the time will not be right for the church to be gathered to Jesus in the rapture until we see these two events come to pass. In chapter 8, I cover a total of six events that must take place before the rapture can occur.

The next verse is John 14:1-3 (NIV): *"Do not let your hearts be troubled. Trust in God; trust also in me. In my Father's house are many rooms, if it were not so, I would have told you. I am going to prepare a place for you. I will come back and take you to be with me, that you also may be where I am."*

This is a great verse full of the promises of God. It has a lot to say to the church, but I will share three points that are relevant to my study. This verse attests to the resurrection of God's people. It says Christ is coming back to receive his elect or saints to himself. It attests to the fact there will be a rapture, but there is no indication of the timing of the rapture in relation to the Great Tribulation.

The next verse is I Corinthians 15:23 (NIV): *"But each in his own turn: Christ, the first fruits; then, when he comes, those who belong to him."*

This verse is quite self-explanatory. Jesus is coming for his bride. There is a rapture on the horizon. It says when he comes, those who belong to him will be resurrected. The ones who belong to him are the Christians and the Jews who have accepted Christ. The Bible says we will each go in his own time. Yet there is still no indication of the rapture event's timing in this verse.

The next text is 1 Corinthians 15:51-58 (NIV*): "Listen, I tell you a mystery: We will not all sleep, but we will all be changed -- in a flash, in the twinkling of an eye, at the last trumpet, for the trumpet will sound, the dead will be raised imperishable, and we will be changed. For the perishable must clothe itself with the imperishable and the mortal with immortality. When the perishable has been clothed with the imperishable, and the mortal with immortality, then the saying that is written will come true: 'Death has been swallowed up in victory.' Where, O death is your victory? Where, O death is your sting? The sting of death is sin, and the power of sin is the law. But thanks be to God! he gives us victory through our Lord Jesus Christ. Therefore, my dear brothers, stand firm. Let nothing move you. Always give yourselves fully to the work of the Lord, because you know that your labor in the Lord is not in vain."*

This is a great portion of Scripture; it not only talks about the rapture but also goes into great detail on how we will be changed into eternal beings. In light of God's grace, it behooves us to give all of our life and strength to the work of the Lord in whatever capacity God calls us.

This Scripture has confused me a bit about the timing of the rapture. Remember, John B. Doe promotes the pre-Tribulation rapture. I am leaning heavily toward a mid-Tribulation rapture even though I would prefer a pre-Tribulation rapture. (Do we not all like the easy way?) This verse gives evidence of a post-Tribulation rapture. Read 1 Corinthians 15:52 (NIV): *"...in a flash, in the twinkling of an eye, at the last trumpet, for the trumpet will sound, the dead will be raised imperishable, and we will be changed."*

The phrase, *"...at the last trumpet...",* begs the question of which last trumpet. The only last trumpet I am aware is the last trumpet listed as one of the seven trumpets of God's wrath. I do not believe we will go through the wrath of God under the category of the seven trumpets. I believe, with study, this inconsistency will be reconciled, for there are too many Scriptures placing the rapture in Revelation 7 before the wrath of God. I would rather stay with an interpretation with which are multiple verses to back it. Later, in chapter 9, I will explain an alternative to the last trumpet and the accompanying inconsistency will go away.

After four years of working on this study, I now lean toward a mid-Tribulation rapture because of the amount of Scriptural support to back up this position, compared to a pre or post-Tribulation rapture. It is necessary to weigh how plain and easy to understand are the verses used to build a doctrinal position. If the Scripture is vague, the position will be like a house of cards

The next verse is 2 Corinthians 5:1-8 (NIV): *"Now we know that if the earthly tent we live in is destroyed, we have a building from God, an eternal house in heaven, not built by human hands. Meanwhile, we groan, longing to be clothed with our heavenly dwelling, because when we are clothed, we will not be found naked. For while we are in this tent, we groan and are burdened, because we do not wish to be unclothed but to be clothed with our heavenly dwelling, so that what is mortal may be swallowed up by life. Now it is God who has made us for this very purpose and has given us the Spirit as a deposit, guaranteeing what is to come. Therefore, we are always confident and know that as long as we are home in the body we are away from the Lord. We live by faith, not by sight. We are confident; I say and would prefer to be away from the body and at home with the Lord."*

These verses attest to the resurrection and the promise of a new eternal body. They give us an expectant hope in the future of exchanging our earthly body for an eternal one that will allow us to live with Christ forever. However, these verses give no indication about the timing of Christ's return or the placement of the rapture even though they give us significant assurance God has better things for us ahead for all eternity.

John B. Doe's next verse, Ephesians 5:27, (NIV), states, *"...and to present her to himself as a radiant church, without stain or wrinkle or any other blemish, but holy and blameless..."* Again, this verse attests to the resurrection of the believer, but there is no mention of the rapture or the timing of Christ's coming.

Next, read Philippians 3:11, (NIV*): "...and so, somehow, to attain to the resurrection from the dead..."* and 3:20-21,(NIV): *"But our citizenship is in heaven. And we eagerly await a Savior from there, the Lord Jesus Christ, who by the power that enables him to bring everything under his control, will transform our lowly bodies so that they will be like his glorious body."*

These verses also speak about the resurrection and our mortal bodies being transformed to be like Christ's glorious body. I can see these verses touching on Christ's power to bring about the rapture, but there is no indication about the timing of this event.

Next, read Colossians 3:4 (NIV): *"When Christ, who is your life, appears, then you also will appear with him in glory."* This verse surely refers to the rapture. It clearly says when Christ appears, we will be in glory with him, but it gives no timing or placement for the rapture.

Then the next verses to look at are 1Thessalonians 2:19, 3:13, 4:13-17, 5:9-23 and 1 Thessalonians 2:19 (NIV): *"For what is our hope, our joy, or the crown in which we will glory in the presence of our Lord Jesus when he comes? Is it not you?"* This verse attests to the resurrection and Christ's coming for us, but again there is no indication of timing.

The next verse is 1 Thessalonians 3:13 (NIV*): "May he strengthen your hearts so you will be blameless and holy in the presence of our God and Father when our Lord Jesus comes with all his holy ones."* This verse points to Christ's coming for his saints, but as with the others, it gives no timing for the rapture.

Going further, 1 Thessalonians 4:13-17 (NIV): says, *"Brothers, we do not want you to be ignorant about those who fall asleep, or to grieve like the rest of men, who have no hope. We believe that Jesus died and rose again and so we believe that God will bring with Jesus those who have fallen asleep in him. According to the Lord's own word, we tell you that we who are still alive at the coming of the Lord, will certainly not precede those who have fallen asleep. For the Lord himself will come down from heaven, with a loud command, with the voice of the archangel and with the trumpet call of God, and the dead in Christ will rise first. After that, we who are still alive and are left will be caught up with them in the clouds to meet the Lord in the air. And so we will be with the Lord forever."* This is a great verse affirming the resurrection of both the dead in Christ and those who are alive at his coming. It is saying when Christ comes, those who are alive will be taken by the rapture and not by death.

The next verse to examine is 2 Thessalonians 5:9-23. I will not write out this whole verse, but all of chapter 5 should be read in this study. This chapter starts out talking about times and dates and being caught unprepared for Christ's coming.

I will, however, quote the first six verses of 1 Thessalonians 5:1-6 (NIV*): "Now, brothers, about times and dates we do not need to write to you, for you know very well that the day of the Lord will come like a thief in the night. While people are saying 'Peace and safety', destruction will come on them suddenly, as labor pains on a pregnant woman, and they will not escape. But you, brothers, are not in darkness so that this day should surprise you like a thief. You are all sons of the light and sons of the day. We do not belong to the night or to the darkness. So then, let us not be like others who are asleep, but let us be alert and self-controlled."*

The church should not be caught by surprise at the coming of the Lord; it is only the unsaved world around us who are crying, "Peace and safety", who will be surprised as if by a thief in the night. Looking at 2 Thessalonians 5 as a whole, is so important in understanding the Lord's coming, yet there is no sign of the timing of the rapture.

John B. Doe's last verses on the rapture are 2 Thessalonians 2:1, 7-8. 2 Thessalonians 2:1 (NIV): says, *"Concern-*
58

ing the coming of our Lord Jesus Christ and our being gathered to him..." This verse attests to Christ's coming and the rapture, but like the other verses fails to provide any indication of timing. One point that needs to be stated though, if you will read the next two verses after 2 Thessalonians 2:1, you will see that Paul is telling the church that the rapture will not happen until certain events take place. The key event is the revealing of antichrist. Therefore this verse in full context gives some support to a mid-tribulation. rapture.

Next, 2 Thessalonians 2:7, 8 (NIV): "*For the secret power of lawlessness is already at work; but the one who now holds it back will continue to do so till he is taken out of the way. And then the lawless one will be revealed, whom the Lord Jesus will overthrow with the breath of his mouth and destroy by the splendor of his coming.*" These last two verses are quite interesting. This verse is generally accepted as referring to the antichrist, and many believe that this verse is talking about the collective power of spirit-filled Christians being able to restrain the antichrist. Therefore, the rapture is looked at as the way that the restrainer would be taken out of the way which would give the antichrist free reign on the earth. If you really think about this explanation and look closely at these Scriptures, you will see a problem with this explanation. Read the portion where it says, "but the one who now holds it back will continue to do so till he is taken out of the way." This verse describes the restrainer as "the one", not a collective force, such as from masses of Christians. I have always had a problem believing that the Christians have to be raptured before the antichrist could have free reign. If the collective force and power of all praying saints could restrain the antichrist, then why did not the prayers and collective power of all Christians restrain Hitler and other tyrants that have lived and attacked Christians and Jews on the earth, including stopping all the Christians from being martyred throughout the ages?

Most Christians, who believe in a pre-Tribulation rapture, also believe there will be Tribulation saints after the rapture, comprised of those who had drifted away from God before the time of the rapture but came back to God after missing that event. As I have come to my conclusion that the rapture will be a mid-Tribulation event, with few exceptions, I do not see any Christians on the earth after the rapture. There is just no Scriptural proof to show this. All who will come back to God or get saved during the early years of the Great Tribulation will have made up their minds to serve God or not, and when the rapture occurs, those who are not Christians will have fully rejected Christ. The reason I bring up this thought is that those who believe there will be tribulation saints would have to infer that tribulation saints would be powerless and not have the power of the Holy Spirit. I just do not see how you can believe that the Holy Spirit is taken out of the earth? The Holy Spirit is God! He is all-present and, I believe, he will be at work during all parts of the Great Tribulation.

I do not mean to come off like a know-it-all, but I believe I have a reasonable explanation for who "he" is that has to be taken out of the way, in order to give the antichrist full reign on the earth. Do you remember the story of when Daniel fasted and prayed for God's intervention? He was visited by the Lord and his top warring angel, Michael the archangel.

Read Daniel 10. Here are a few good verses to concider: First, Daniel 10:12, 13 (KJV): *"Then said he unto me, fear not, Daniel: for from the first day that thou didst set thine heart to understand and to chasten thyself before thy God, thy words were heard, and I am come for thy words. But the prince of the kingdom of Persia withstood me one and twenty days: but, lo, Michael, one of the chief princes, came to help me; and I remained there with the kings of Persia."*

Next read Daniel 10:20, 21 (KJV): *"Then said he, Knowest thou wherefore I am come unto thee? And now will I return to fight with the prince of Persia: and when I am gone forth, lo, the prince of Grecia shall come. But I will shew thee that which is noted in the scriptures of truth: and there is none that holdeth with me in these things, but Michael your prince."* So my explanation for this verse is that one of God's most powerful angels, Michael, is the one who is holding the antichrist at bay until it is time for satan to unleash his full fury of evil on the earth, and he, Michael, will have to be taken out of the way or be told to halt his restraining work, not the church. I would have to say that the only verse that shows the timing of the rapture as pre-Tribulation is this one here. Yet, if you agree that the church through the ages has not really been a restraining force with the power to stop evil, then you may conclude as I have that this Scripture does not provide Scriptural proof that the rapture will happen before the antichrist is revealed or before the Great Tribulation starts. I will be going into greater detail on Michael the Archangel in a later chapter, showing in greater detail why I believe that Michael is the restrainer who must be removed or told to stand down.

David G. Doe

I will now look at David G. Doe's view on the pre-Tribulation rapture. Most of what I will discuss concerning his views will be from his book, Triumphant Return. In a section of his book called, "Biblical support for a pre-Tribulation rapture", his first sentence says, "The Scriptures clearly support a pre-Tribulation rapture of believers." Please understand my motives in examining David G. Doe's teachings. I have come to a point where I just do not see the pre-Tribulation viewpoint of the rapture clearly supported by Scripture. Yet Mr. D. Doe says the pre-Tribulation viewpoint is clearly supported.

However, I see the mid-Tribulation view of the rapture clearly supported. Some people might ask, "Just what difference does it really make?" If it did not make any difference, I would not be writing this, but it will make a huge difference when the Great Tribulation starts and millions of believers realize the rapture did not happen. They will be upset at their Bible teachers and pastors who misled them. Please do not take offense at this last statement. I would love for a Bible teacher or pastor to show me clear Scriptural support to a pre-Tribulation rapture, but because Mr. Doe's views and my views on the timing of the rapture are so opposed, I have to examine them to see which view really is clearly supported by the Word of God.

Mr. D. Doe goes on to cover five reasons for believing that the rapture is a pre-Tribulation event. I will examine each of these five Scriptural texts and his position in this context. I will also look at these compared to my position that has evolved into being a mid-Tribulation rapture position. You can decide for yourself which position is clearly supported by the Word of God.

The first Scripture David G. Doe uses to support the pre-Tribulation position is Revelation 19:11, 14 (KJV): *"And I saw heaven opened, and behold a white horse; and he that sat upon him was called Faithful and True, and in righteousness he doth judge and make war."* Also, *"The armies which were in heaven followed him upon white horses, clothed in fine linen, white and clean."* If we look at the context of the text, we will notice it is the nineteenth chapter of Revelation. The wrath of God is finished and Christ is returning with his saints. Mr. D. Doe states, the saints have to go to heaven before this event happens in order for the saints to come back to the earth with Jesus from heaven. I agree with this statement, but Mr. D. Doe does not address the fact that if the rapture is a mid-Tribulation event, as shown in the second half of Revelation 7, before the wrath of God starts in Revelation 8, then it can be seen the mid-Tribulation position would place the saints in heaven in more than enough time to return with Christ as indicated in Revelation 19. Instead, Mr. D. Doe makes a reference to the fact that a post-Tribulation position is not logical. I agree with Mr. D. Doe on this point; because, the post-Tribulation position states the rapture does not happen until the end of Gods wrath. I agree, Scripture does not support the post-Tribulation rapture position. The main point I would like to make is, his first Scriptural support for a pre-Tribulation rapture does not contradict the mid-Tribulation position. Therefore, the Word of God is not clearly supporting a pre-Tribulation rapture from this Scripture verse.

David G. Doe's second argument for a pre-Tribulation rapture is from Revelation 7. Mr. D. Doe points out how the four angels who have power to harm the earth are told to hold back until the 144,000 Jews are sealed. He then goes on to say that if there is no sealing of Christians to protect them, then they must be already raptured; therefore, on that basis, he sees the rapture as a pre-Tribulation event. If you read Revelation 7, where the 144,000 are sealed, the rapture from the mid-Tribulation view occurs sometime after the sealing of the 144,000 in Revelation 7, but before the wrath of God is poured out in Revelation chapter 8.

What is interesting is that Mr. D. Doe states, the sealing of the 144,000 is before God's wrath; because, it shows that God never pours his wrath upon the righteous. Check this out, at the point of the sealing of the 144,000, the six seals of Revelation 6 have already been opened. In this case, Mr. D. Doe is saying the seals are not the wrath of God. At other times he has said the seals are the wrath of God. I will give further reasoning why the seals are not part of the wrath of God in chapter 8. The mid-Tribulation view I share in this study goes on to say the saints or the church will go through the opening of the seals of Revelation 6. Then the 144,000 Jews will be sealed in Revelation 7, and after the sealing of the 144,000, the mid-Tribulation rapture will take place before the wrath of God begins in Revelation 8. Again, Mr. D. Doe's second argument for a pre-Tribulation rapture does not conflict with the mid-Tribulation view; therefore, the second Scripture verse does not clearly support the pre-Tribulation view of the rapture.

David G. Doe's third argument for a pre-Tribulation rapture is that the restrainer must be taken out of the way. He uses 2 Thessalonians 2: 6-8 (NIV): *"And now you know what is holding him back, so that he may be revealed at the proper time. For the secret power of lawlessness is already at work; but the one who now holds it back will continue to do so till he is taken out of the way. And then the lawless one will be revealed, whom the Lord Jesus will overthrow with the breath of his mouth and destroy by the splendor of his coming."* When you read this Scripture carefully, you will see the antichrist cannot be revealed until the restrainer is taken out of the way. So if the restrainer is the church or the saints on earth, then the antichrist cannot be revealed until after the rapture of the church. When you read 2 Thessalonians 2:1-3 (NIV) you really have a problem: *"Concerning the coming of our Lord Jesus Christ and our being gathered to him, we ask you brothers not to become easily unsettled or alarmed by some prophecy, report or letter supposed to have come from us, saying that the day of the Lord has already come. Don't let anyone deceive you in any way, for that day will not come until the rebellion occurs and the man of lawlessness is revealed, the man doomed to destruction."* This Scripture says before the church can be gathered to him, the antichrist has to first be revealed. This totally contradicts 2 Thessalonians 2:6-8.

That text says that the restrainer must be removed first. Which is it? You cannot have it both ways. If the restrainer is not the church, the problem goes away. I cover this contradiction later in this study, pointing out it makes more sense that the restrainer is not the church but is Michael the Archangel, who is the chief warring angel who came to Daniel's aid when Daniel had prayed and fasted for twenty-one days. But the bottom line is David G. Doe's third Scripture is not clearly supporting a pre-Tribulation rapture.

David G. Doe's last two points are handled as one, so I will try to cover them as one. First, he says, *"The Lord commands the church to always be watchful for Christ's coming."* Then he goes on to say, *"...which could happen at any time..."*, quoting 1 Thessalonians 5:6 and Luke 12:40. *"Therefore let us not sleep, as do others, but let us watch and be sober."* Then it says, *"Be ye therefore ready also: for the Son of Man cometh at an hour when ye think not."* As I look at 1 Thessalonians 5:6 where it says "...but let us watch...", my question is, "If the Lord's coming and the rapture are without warning, why do we have to watch?" If we are told to watch, there has to be something for which to watch. Furthermore, if there is something for which we are to watch, then how can you say that the rapture is an imminent event? For an event to be imminent, by definition, there cannot be anything that has to happen before that imminent event. If there is anything that has to happen, for which we have to watch and wait, then that event is not imminent.

What is interesting is that David G. Doe teaches that the rapture has been an imminent event for two thousand years. My question is, "If we had to wait for Israel to be reborn as a nation, which happened in 1948, then how could the rapture have been imminent before 1948?" Also, the apostle Paul talks about the Lord's coming and our gathering to him as not taking place until the man of lawlessness is revealed. Read 2 Thessalonians 2:1-3 (NIV): *"Concerning the coming of the Lord Jesus Christ and our being gathered to him, we ask you, brothers, not to become easily unsettled or alarmed by some prophecy, report or letter supposed to have come from us, saying that the day of the Lord has come. Don't let anyone deceive you in any way, for that day will not come until the rebellion occurs and the man of lawlessness is revealed, the man doomed to destruction."* So how can anyone say the rapture is Imminent if the man of lawlessness is not revealed? Does it not make sense that the rapture will not be imminent until after the antichrist is revealed? There other events that must also take place before the rapture. I will discuss this in chapter 8.

Some people say no man knows the day or the hour of the Lord's return. I agree with this, as this is what the Bible says. But once the antichrist is revealed, we will still not know the day or the hour of Christ's return. It will be time for us to obey the words in Luke 21:25-28 (NIV*): "There will be signs in the sun, moon and stars, on the earth; nations will be in anguish and perplexity at the roaring of the sea. Men will faint from terror, apprehensive of what is coming on the world, for heavenly bodies will be shaken. At that time, they will see the Son of Man coming in a cloud with power and great glory. When these things begin to take place, stand up and lift up your heads, because your redemption is drawing near."* If we have to wait for these things to begin to come to pass, and if we have been commanded to watch for these things, then how can you say the rapture is imminent?

In closing, on page one hundred eighty-eight of David G. Doe's book <u>Triumphant Return,</u> he says, "...the <u>Webster's Nineth New Collegiate Dictionary,</u> defines 'imminent' as ready to take place, especially hanging threateningly over one's head." He continues to say, "As my colleague,

Ronald noted in his book, <u>Maranatha Our Lord, Come!</u>, "Other things may happen before the imminent event, but nothing else MUST take place before it happens...If something else must take place before an event can happen, that event cannot be counted as imminent."

What more can I say? David G. Doe goes on to say that because the rapture is pre-Tribulation, it has to be imminent, but that statement is based on flawed Scriptural support. But if the rapture is a mid-Tribulation event, then the rapture cannot be imminent until the Great Tribulation is in motion and the 144,000 are sealed and the antichrist arrives, and other events take place that I will discuss later in chapter 8. Again David G. Doe's last scriptural argument does not clearly support a pre-Tribulation rapture.

Reverend Philip Doe

I was not planning on covering any teaching from Rev. Philip Doe, but while watching Rev.P. Doe, the other night on cable television talk about the rapture and commenting that there are a lot of people teaching the church is going through the Great Tribulation, he said, "Let me shoot that down right here." When he said that, I was all ears. At the time I started this study, I had a lot of questions on the timing of the rapture. I had always held to the pre-Tribulation view of the rapture. It was my hope when I started this study, I would find the Scriptural strength from the Word of God to show me the pre-Tribulation view is the correct view. However, as this study progressed, the opposite has happened. I am now convinced the mid-Tribulation rapture is the most accurate interpretation, based on the weight of God's word. So when Rev. P. Doe said, "...let me shoot the mid-Tribulation rapture teaching down right here...", he had my attention. Thank God for a DVR on my television. I record my favorite evangelists every day so that I can listen to them on my schedule. I started playing Rev.

P. Doe's teachings about why the rapture is pre-Tribulation several times. I dug out several Bibles to check his Bible quotations, and this is what I found.

Rev. P. Doe starts out by saying that the first three chapters of Revelation talk about the seven churches of Asia, and after that, the church is not mentioned again until the end of the book of Revelation. He then asked why. He responded, "...Because, the church goes up in the air!" Then he goes on to say, "In the fourth chapter, John is snatched up into heaven, and he sees the twenty-four elders who were seated, robed, and crowned." He used the phrase, "Snatched up into heaven." But this is not what the Bible states. This phrase makes it sound as if this is a rapture event occurring here, in reality, it simply says, "...Come up here". When it is time for the rapture, God will not be asking us to come up, for without notice, in the twinkling of an eye, we will be "...caught up..." We will not be asked to come up.

Another point that Rev. P. Doe makes is, because the elders are wearing robes and crowns, this represents the church with white robes and crowns. I see a problem with this interpretation. First, you do not read of a multitude in heaven that would represent the saints or the church in heaven in white robes until Revelation 7:9 (NIV): *After this I looked, and there before me was a great multitude that no one could count, from every tribe, people, and language standing before the throne and in front of the Lamb. They were wearing white robes and were holding palm branches in their hands.* If you read this carefully, you will notice at this time in the book of Revelation, it does not mention this multitude as having crowns. Why? A good explanation for this is the saints will not be given crowns until the Judgment Seat of Christ for believers takes place. It is reasonable to believe this judgment of believers will not happen until all of the saints are in heaven. So if the saints are being martyred in Revelation 6, the rewards will not be

68

handed out until all these saints are united in heaven. Reverend John B. Doe puts this judgment of believers during the time when God is pouring out his wrath on the earth. Reverend John B. Doe then concludes that the Marriage Supper of the Lamb happens after the Judgment Seat of Christ. This makes sense to me.

If the saints and the church have to wait to receive their rewards until all the saints are in heaven, then how can you say the elders in Revelation 4 represent the church wearing their crowns? Therefore, when it speaks of the elders in Revelation 4 wearing crowns, it has to refer only to the twenty-four elders. They would be in heaven before the rapture and could have already received their crowns that represent the rewards for what they did with their lives on earth. I have read that many people believe the twenty-four elders are leaders from the twelve tribes of Israel and the twelve disciples. This makes sense to me, but some people say they would not be in heaven around the Throne until the rapture of the church. I can see two Scriptural reasons why they can be there before the rapture of the church.

The first reason is found in Matthew 27:51-52 (NIV): These verses are talking about what happens when Christ died on the cross and was later resurrected. It says, *"At that moment, the curtain of the temple was torn in two from top to bottom. The earth shook and the rocks split. The tombs broke open and the bodies of many holy people who had died were raised to life."* These holy people were resurrected after Christ was resurrected, and they were seen by many people. Also, if God chose to take Enoch and Elijah to heaven before they died, and if God resurrected these holy people at the time of Christ's resurrection, then it is not a violation of Scripture to imagine God could resurrect the twenty-four elders before the church is resurrected at the rapture.

The second reason is found in Revelation 7:13-14 (NIV): *"Then one of the elders asked me, 'These in white robes -- who are they, and where did they come from?' I answered, 'Sir, you know.' And he said, 'These are they who have come out of the Great Tribulation...'"* Revelation 7:9 says a great multitude in white robes suddenly appeared in heaven. I see this plainly describing the rapture. So how can the elders represent the church in Revelation 4 if the multitude in white robes do not appear in heaven until Revelation 7:9? They do not represent the church; they are just the twenty-four elders who are at the throne of God when the church arrives in Revelation 7.

Then Reverend Philip Doe says the church is raptured in Revelation 4 and the antichrist shows up in Revelation 6. He goes on to say that "If 4 comes before 6, then we are out of here. If you want to stay, that's your business." But consider the wording of 2 Thessalonians 2:1-4, (NIV): *"Concerning the coming of our Lord Jesus Christ and our being gathered to him, we ask you, brothers, not to become easily unsettled or alarmed by some prophecy, report or letter supposed to have come from us, saying that the day of the Lord has already come. Do not let anyone deceive you in any way, for that day will not come until the rebellion occurs and the man of lawlessness is revealed, the man doomed to destruction. He opposes and exalts himself over everything that is called God or is worshiped, and even sets himself up in God's temple, proclaiming himself to be God."*

Here we see clear wording. Paul is teaching the rapture, or as Paul says, "...the gathering to him....", will not take place until the antichrist is revealed. If the antichrist is not revealed in Revelation 4, and he is not revealed until Revelation 6, then the rapture cannot happen until sometime after this event happens in Revelation 6. Based on the Word of God, I cannot agree with Reverend Philip Doe.

7. The Coming Antichrist

When I first wrote the outline for this study, I included a chapter on the antichrist. Well, as this study was taking shape, I felt all I would be writing concerning the antichrist would be a rehash of what everyone else has been saying. I felt unless I had something fresh to write, I should just drop this topic from my study. A few weeks later, as I was finishing the last chapter, things started to change my mind about writing the chapter on the antichrist. As I was reading the book of Revelation, two fresh truths jumped out at me. As I studied further to confirm if I was seeing the Word of God correctly, I had further insights jumping out at me. At that point, I realized I had to write this chapter.

To begin with, I must set the stage for where I believe the antichrist appears on the world's stage. If you will read the following verses, I will explain where I am going with this. Read Revelation 13:1-3 (NIV): *"And I saw a beast coming out of the sea. He had ten horns and seven heads, with ten crowns on his horns, and on each head a blasphemous name. The beast I saw resembled a leopard, but had feet like those of a bear and a mouth like that of a lion. The dragon gave the beast his power and his throne and great authority. One of the heads of the beast seemed to have had a fatal wound, but the fatal wound had been healed. The whole world was astonished and followed the beast."*

I do not pretend to understand all that is written in these verses, but what I do understand I will explain. When these verses start off talking about a beast coming out of the sea with ten horns, ten crowns, and seven heads, it is a bit confusing, but what we can see is the beast is a rising government that will grow to become a One-World Government. It goes on to say one of the heads of the beast seemed to have had a fatal wound. What I saw in this verse is the antichrist will come from one of the heads of the beast. What is interesting is, before one of the heads of the beast is wounded, the whole being described here as the beast with ten horns (or ten leaders or heads of state) must be fully in place. Once the antichrist comes from one of the heads of the beast, then the antichrist is referred to as "the beast". If you read the following verses, it will help clarify the description of the beast that becomes a world government of ten kings or leaders. Read Revelation 17:12 and 14 (NIV): *"The ten horns you saw are ten kings who have not yet received a kingdom, but who for one hour will receive authority as kings along with the beast. They will make war against the Lamb, but the Lamb will overcome them because he is Lord of lords and King of kings - and with him will be his called, chosen and faithful followers."*

Let me explain some more about the coming antichrist. There have been many world leaders who have had the spirit of antichrist, but just having the spirit of antichrist does not make them the antichrist. Hitler certainly had the spirit of antichrist, but he was not the antichrist. If you believe as I do that the man who will become the antichrist is alive on the earth today, you have to realize even though he is destined to become the antichrist, he will not be the antichrist until satan literally possesses his body and brings him back from death.

Now if we draw from the accepted teaching of the coming antichrist, you will see most prophetic teachers teach that the man who will become the antichrist will be the leader of this One-World-Government, and then this world leader will be mortally wounded. Many believe he will have a mortal head wound, and his miraculous recovery will usher in the antichrist. Now go back and read Revelation 13:3 (NIV): *"One of the heads of the beast seemed to have had a fatal wound, but the fatal wound had been healed."* **This verse does not say the leader of this One-World Government will be wounded. NO!! It says one of the <u>heads</u> of this government will be wounded. This means to qualify as a candidate for the antichrist, you must be one of the ten heads.** Let me further explain. The European Union is getting ready to elect a permanent leader to lead the countries or regions that are aligned with this new One-World Government. Tony Blair, the former leader of England, is one of the leaders who has tossed his hat into the ring to run for this position. I have already heard of Bible teachers who believe that Tony Blair is going to be the antichrist. But, no, this is not what is being said in the Bible. **The Bible says one of the ten heads is fatally wounded, not the leader of the ten heads.**

An important point to understand is, the event that leads to one of the ten heads of state being fatally wounded cannot occur until the One World Governments is in place. This means that according to 2Thessalonians 2:1-3, the gathering of believers or the rapture cannot occur until the antichrist is revealed, and the One World Government is in place.

Many Bible teachers are now saying the future One-World Government will not be comprised of ten nations but ten <u>regions</u> of the world. The ten crowns and ten horns represent ten leadership positions, this verse says one of the heads is wounded with a fatal wound which means the leader over the ten heads or the president of the European Union does not qualify to become the antichrist. He must be one of the heads of the beast to qualify. Now if you think about this, any one of these ten horns or heads of state that comprise the new One-World Government could end up being the antichrist. This means that we will not know for certain who the antichrist is until one of the heads of state is fatally wounded.

Now this leads to another interesting thought. If any one of the heads that comprise the One-World Government can be tapped to become the antichrist, then the following thought gets very interesting. I only know of one end-times teacher, Dr Jack Van Impe, who has said our current president is being groomed to be "The Man". I have said all along I just do not see how he could be "The Man", but personally, I do not know of any leader who is more qualified. Now, if you are following my reasoning here, you may come to the same conclusion as I. If the United States becomes the North American Region of the New-World Government, and its leader is the President, then the President would become one of the heads of the beast. This would make the President of the United States a qualifying person, who could become the antichrist. WOW! What a thought.

Another important thought to keep in mind as these events start to unfold is, BEFORE the United States would be willing to sign up and join the One-World Government and become part of the North American Region of this global government, the United States has to fall apart economically, along with a complete breakdown of society as we know it. A period of time from between six months to a year on the short side and up to two to three years on the long side could occur before we would be willing to give up our independence. We might see events like terrorist attacks on our cities, hyper-inflation, and the collapse of our dollar, food shortages, famine, and anarchy in our cities. This stretch of time will seem like the end-of-the-world to many. Many Christians will believe the Great Tribulation has started. This period of time is only part of the birth pains that will be coming on the world before the Great Tribulation begins, merely setting the stage for the antichrist to come to power. Personally, I believe this period, before the Great Tribulation starts, will be on the short side of my predicttions. Once things start falling together, world events will move rapidly to the prophetic destiny of the Lord's return.

Imagine how these coming events will affect our lives. This coming time of upheaval will be a window of time that will last from the time the world economies collapse until the ten-region One-World Government is formed. This window will be unlike any time in American history. Life as we know it will be over. This special window will last until the antichrist comes to power. We need to be ready to take advantage of the greatest evangelistic opportunity the world has ever seen. People's lives will be turned upside down. Churches will be filled with people looking for answers. If we know this time is coming, we can prepare to have a part in this great harvest of souls. Once the antichrist comes to power, this open window to share Christ's love will soon close.

Recently, as I was preparing this study for the printers, I was watching a well-known televangelist from Texas. He was talking about the soon coming collapse of the dollar and America's economic collapse. He made the statement that he knows when this is going to happen. He then predicted that America's dollar and economy would collapse when the church is raptured out of here. This statement is giving a false sense of security to all his followers. If you recognize from this study that the One-World Government has to be in place before the Great Tribulation starts, then you realize that the church will see a period of tribulation, even if the rapture were a pre-Tribulation event. I would not want to be in the shoes of this preacher when the US economy collapses and his church fills up with all these people who are asking him, "Where is the rapture that is supposed to get us out of here?" The store shelves have been emptied from panic buying and these people are not ready for what lies ahead. In fact, I believe most of the churches in America are not ready for what lies ahead.

If you have followed me this far, you will realize this One-World Government will have a leader who does not become the antichrist. This global government will probably be faltering, and the stage will be set for a greater leader to rise from its ranks. Then when one of the heads of the beast or one of the leaders of this ten-nation One-World Government is fatally wounded and lies at death's door, he will be brought back to the land of the living. He will arise with the wisdom and the cunning of satan. He will show the world he is the one they are to follow. Read, Revelation 13:3 (NIV): *"One of the heads of the beast seemed to have had a fatal wound, but the fatal wound had been healed. The whole world was astonished and followed the beast."*

Another verse that helps to understand the nature and makeup of the beast is found in Daniel 7:20-21 (NIV): *"I also wanted to know about the ten horns on its head and about the other horn that came up, before which three of them fell - the horn that looked more imposing than the others and that had eyes and a mouth that spoke boastfully. As I watched, this horn was waging war against the saints and defeating them."* The portion of this verse that says, "The horn that looked more imposing than the others", is a phrase that gives evidence that one of the ten horns will rise up from the others to become the antichrist. Once this horn or head of state has been fatally wounded, he will come back as satan in the flesh, and then it will be evident who the antichrist is.

If you study the Scriptures, you will come to realize there is one sure way to know who the antichrist is before his coming to power. The Bible says he who has wisdom may be able to figure it out. Revelation 13:18 (KJV) says, *"Here is wisdom. Let him that hath understanding count the num-*

ber of the beast: for it is the number of a man; and his number is Six hundred threescore and six." Think about this, if the antichrist were to be the leader of the European Union, such as Tony Blair, it does not take any wisdom at all to figure out who the antichrist is – the president of the European Union. However, if you try to figure out which of these ten horns or leaders is to be the antichrist, you would need to see all of these leaders' birth certificates so that you could see the name with which they were born. One prominent world leader that could someday be one of the ten leaders of this New World Government, his birth certificate is not available for anyone to see.

With the study of Daniel 7, you will see some hints as to what kind of leader the antichrist will be. These hints could help discern who out of the ten world leaders will be the antichrist. The first hint is found in Daniel 7:20b (NIV): *"...the horn that looked more imposing then the others and that had eyes and a mouth that spoke boastfully."* This verse says this leader will be imposing in stature, boastful and arrogant. Unfortunately many world leaders match this description. Then read Daniel 7:25a (NIV): *"He will speak against the Most High and oppress his saints and try to change the set times and the laws."* This leader will be a leader who will bring in many changes to customs and established laws." An important point to think about is, because a One-World Government must be in place before one of the ten heads of state can be fatally wounded, and this has to happen before the antichrist can rise to power. This seriously puts the imminent return of the Lord on hold until a One-World Government is in place.

Next, I want to point out that we have been misled concerning the kind of mortal wound this world leader would have. As I mentioned earlier, most Christians believe the world leader would recover from a fatal head wound. This is taken from Revelation 13:3a (NIV): *"One of the heads of the*

77

beast seemed to have had a fatal wound, but the fatal wound had been healed." **This verse does not say this leader will recover from a head wound. No, what it is saying is one of the ten heads of the beast is fatally wounded. What does "one of the heads" mean? What it means is the beast is comprised of a number of leaders or heads of state, and one of these ten heads of state is fatally wounded but not necessarily from a wound to the head.** Why is this important? I believe this event will reveal the antichrist and the beginning of the Great Tribulation will soon follow. If most Christians have been taught the antichrist would arise from the miraculous recovery from a fatal head wound, then when this leader does not recover from a head wound but maybe from a fatal wound to other vital organs, this will leave many confused. They will not know if this really is the antichrist. Then when the antichrist rises to deceive even the elect if possible, he will have confused Christians who are open to be deceived.

Another point that could lead to confusion concerning who the antichrist is, could arise from the type of wound that this world leader receives. I have heard teaching that this leader who is fatally wounded will be wounded from a sword. The Bible does say he is wounded with a sword. (Revelation 13:14b, KJV) *"...saying to them that dwell on the earth, that they should make an image to the beast, which had the wound by a sword and did live."* The point I would like to make is, when John the Revelator wrote this they did not have the weapons like we have today. When my wife and I traveled across the country doing Kids Crusades, we did a message on the whole armor of God. We substituted modern weapons for the weapons used by a Roman soldier back in Bible days. For the Sword of the Spirit, we substituted a rifle. Now it is possible the future antichrist will be wounded with a sword, but I do not believe we should be adamant about what type of weapon will be used. John the Revelator had never seen a rifle.

78

8. Pre. vs. mid-Tribulation view of the rapture and the weight of Scripture

For most of my thirty-eight years as a Christian, I have held to the pre-Tribulation view of the rapture and know this position quite well. When I started this chapter, I had no idea it would grow to the size it has. This chapter could be divided into three chapters. What I have decided to do is divide this chapter into three parts.

First, I will do a comparative study of some of the best Scriptural reasons for believing in the pre-Tribulation rapture, and then show an alternative view for each, that would support a mid-Tribulation rapture.

Secondly, I will cover seven Bible-backed events that must take place in the last generation before the rapture can happen. Only one of these events has happened to date.

Thirdly, I will do a study from the book of Daniel that clearly shows that the rapture will be a mid-Tribulation event.

I have covered some of this material in other chapters of this book, but this is where the pieces of the puzzle are really coming together. I believe some repetition helps in the learning process, helping us form a sound conclusion from the study of God's Word. A challenge I would like to make to the readers of this chapter is to first, have an open mind. Then, either prove my conclusions to be wrong with sound arguments from the Word of God, or shout my conclusions from the housetops. There can be no middle ground. To be wrong on this doctrine would leave the church ill-prepared for what we will face leading up to the Lord's return.

Part One:
Pre-Tribulation vs. Mid- Tribulation Comparison

1. The restrainer must be removed

I am going to start off with one of the most common Scriptural verses that scholars who believe in the pre-Tribulation rapture use to support this view point. It is found in 2 Thessalonians 2:7-8a (NIV): *"For the secret power of lawlessness is already at work; but the one who now holds it back will continue to do so till he is taken out of the way. And then the lawless one will be revealed."*

The reason this verse is so important to the pre-Tribulation position, (which states that the Holy Spirit or the Spirit filled church is the restrainer that holds back the coming reign of the antichrist.) Is because; those holding this position believe that as long as the church is on the earth with the indwelling Holy Spirit in us, then the Holy Spirit's power in us will restrain the antichrist from fully rising to power. **I have mentioned earlier in this study that I see a weakness in this interpretation; because, I do not see either Scriptural or actual evidence that the Spirit-filled believers have been able to restrain evil on the earth. We could not restrain Hitler or the evil of other tyrannical leaders of the past. When the saints were being tortured in Rome, Spirit-filled Christians could not stop the martyrdom of the saints, so why do we think we have the power to hold back the antichrist now?**

I would like to propose a question to help solve a second problem with God having to remove the church in order to keep us from preventing the antichrist's rise to power. "Does God answer all our prayers affirmatively?" No! God answers our prayers if they are in God's will. If we pray for something outside of the will of God, he will not grant our petition. When you think about the greatest attacks in history against those whom God loves, you realize these attacks always have led to great victories. Without the enslavement of the Israelites in Egypt, we would not have seen the exodus. Without the persecution of eighty thousand Christians by Chairman Mao in China, there would not be one to two hundred million Christians in China today. Without Hitler and the Holocaust, Israel would not have been reborn as a nation. Without the Crucifixion of Christ, we would not have our salvation. Without the coming of the antichrist, we would not have the coming of the Lord. The question I would like to pose is, "Would it have been possible, through prayer, to have stopped these events from happening?" We know from God's Word that Jesus had to go to the cross; this event could not be stopped. I do not believe these other events were supposed to be stopped. I believe during extraordinary times of persecution, the church and believers are to pray for personal intervention and protection. During these times, believers need to pray for the salvation of people our lives touch. We need to look at these times of tribulation as opportunities to win the lost and accomplish God's will.

Before it is time for the Lord to come back, will it be God's will for the antichrist to come to power? The answer is yes. So, if it is God's will for the antichrist to come to power, why would God answer our prayers to prevent the antichrist from coming to power? Therefore, if God is not going to answer prayers that are contrary to his will concerning the antichrist, then why would God have to remove the church for this reason? Yet if removing the church is the correct interpretation of this verse, then where is the weight of other Scriptures to back it? To the best of my knowledge, they are totally absent.

Now the next question is, "If we have been misinterpreting this Scripture, what would be an alternative interpretation, and does that view have the strong weight of Scripture to back it?" I will now give a Scripturally-backed alternative as to why I believe the first position I have discussed is wrong. The alternative position that keeps getting stronger as I study this is that the restrainer referred to here is Michael, God's chief warring angel. Jude 9 refers to Michael as the archangel. Webster's dictionary says an archangel is an angel of high rank.

After Daniel had fasted and prayed for twenty-one days, he had an encounter with the Lord, and an angel told him it took all those days to break through spiritual battles. Daniel 10:13 (NIV) describes this experience. *"But the prince of the Persian kingdom resisted me twenty-one days. Then Michael, one of the chief princes, came to help me, because I was detained there with the king of Persia."*

This verse is saying Michael is one of God's top warring angels who can step in to help us when we call out to God for help. Plus, Michael has the power to restrain evil. To me, this is compelling, but is there the weight from other Scriptures to back up this idea? Read Daniel 12:1 (NIV): *"At that time, Michael, the great prince who protects your people, will arise. There will be a time of distress such as has not happened from the beginning of nations until then."*

This is a very compelling verse. First, it talks about Michael, the Great Prince who protects God's people. From whom is Michael protecting God's people? Spiritual forces of wickedness undoubtedly. Then notice the context here is during the time of the end. **Now, if Michael, one of God's generals who commands the armies of God, can protect us from evil forces, then does it not make sense that if God wants to allow the forces of evil to rise up on the**

earth in the person of the antichrist, that God could tell Michael, one of his top Generals, to stand-down?

During World War II, we had a few top generals who commanded the U.S. armed forces. One was General MacArthur in the Pacific theater of the war, and another was General Patton commanding the Third Army in Europe. When the war against the Germans and the Japanese was coming to a close, both of these generals wanted to press onward. General MacArthur wanted to roll into China and prevent it from being a future problem, and General Patton wanted to continue to roll into Russia and stop the threat of communism under Stalin. Well, when push came to shove, they had a Commander-in-Chief they had to obey. The President of the United States told both of these generals to stand-down. So does it not make sense that God can tell his leading general, Michael, "the restrainer of evil", to stand-down?

There is another story to illustrate this point. I saw a Disney movie one time where a bear cub was out on its own, and a great lion was stalking the little bear. When the bear cub saw the lion, he became bold and rose up to stand against this great beast. All of a sudden, you could see the look of fear on the lion, who ran away. Then they showed the huge mother bear standing tall behind the little bear cub. It was not the cub after all, that made the lion flee. It was the mother that was backing the cub up that put fear into the lion. It is almost like the church thinks we are the ones who can hold the antichrist back; but no, it is the armies of God under Michael the Archangel's command, who are holding back the powers of evil.

Again, do we have the weight of Scripture to support this argument? There are so many stories in the Bible about angels executing God's judgment and being instruments of delivering God's children when they sought God for help.

83

The first verse I will show is found in the story of Sodom and Gomorrah, Genesis 19:12-13 (NIV*): "The two men said to Lot, 'Do you have anyone else here, sons in law, sons or daughters, or anyone else in the city that belong to you? Get them out of here, because we are going to destroy this place. The outcry to the Lord against its people is so great he has sent us to destroy it."* These men were angels.

Another example, God sent an angel of judgment against Jerusalem and later told this angel to stand-down. Read 1 Chronicles 21:15 (NIV): *"And God sent an angel to destroy Jerusalem, but as the angel was doing so, the Lord saw it and was grieved because of the calamity and said to the angel who was destroying the people, 'Enough! Withdraw your hand."* Another example is in 2 Chronicles when Hezekiah put his trust in the Lord to fight his battles, and when God answered Hezekiah's prayer, the Lord sent angels to fight the forces of evil. The passage in 2 Chronicles 32:7-8 (NIV) says, *"Be strong and courageous. Do not be afraid or discouraged because of the king of Assyria and the vast army with him, for there is a greater power with us than with him. With him is only the arm of the flesh, but with us is the Lord our God to help us and to fight our battles."*

This next verse shows how God answered their prayers for help. In 2 Chronicles 32:20-21 (NIV): the Word says, *"King Hezekiah and the prophet, Isaiah, son of Amoz, cried out in prayer to heaven about this. And the Lord sent an angel who annihilated all the fighting men and the leaders and officers in the camp of the Assyrian king."* In 2 Kings, there are a couple of examples that show what kind of help is available when we seek God's help and intervention. The first is found in 2 Kings 6:15-17 (NIV): *"When the servant of the man of God got up and went out early the next morning, an army with horses and chariots had surrounded the city. 'Oh my Lord, what shall we do?' the servant asked.*

'Don't be afraid,' the prophet answered. 'Those who are with us are more than those who are with them.' And Elisha prayed, 'O Lord open his eyes so he may see.' Then the Lord opened his eyes and he looked and saw the hills full of horses and chariots of fire all around Elisha."

Next, read what happens to their enemies when God fights the battles for us in 2 Kings 19:35 (NIV): *"That night the angel of the Lord went out and put to death a hundred and eighty-five thousand men in the Assyrian camp. When the people got up the next morning, there were all dead bodies!"* Also, let us not forget about the apostles who were thrown into prison for their witness for Jesus. When they were thrown into prison, angels came to their rescue as spoken of in Acts 5:18-19 (NIV*): "They arrested the apostles and put them in the public jail. But during the night an angel of the Lord opened the doors of the jail and brought them out."*

God's word even says in the last days, at the time of the Lord's return, God will send angels to protect us from anyone who tries to harm us. What a promise in God's word! It says in 2 Thessalonians 1:6-7 (NIV), *"God is just: he will pay back trouble to those who trouble you and give relief to you who are troubled, and to us as well. This will happen when the Lord Jesus is revealed from heaven in blazing fire with his powerful angels."*

I see far more weight in the Word of God, showing angels are the powers God uses to restrain. It is not the church that is the restrainer who is keeping the antichrist from coming to power, but it is the armies of God commanded by God's general, Michael, the Archangel. The day is soon coming when the Commander in Chief will issue the order for the armies of God to stand-down. When that day comes, Michael may not want to go along with it, but he will stand–down, and all hell will break loose on the earth.

85

I have to wonder if the following verses in the Bible that I have pondered for a long time could have something to do with what I have been describing here. Read Revelation 12:12b (NIV): *"But woe to the earth and the sea, because the devil has gone down to you! He is filled with fury, because he knows that his time is short."* It gets even more convincing when you go back a few verses and read Revelation 12:7-9 (NIV): "And there was war in heaven. Michael and his angels fought against the dragon, and the dragon and his angels fought back. But they were not strong enough, and they lost their place in heaven. The great dragon was hurled down, that ancient serpent, called the devil or satan, who leads the whole world astray. He was hurled to the earth, and his angels with him." Now if you will skip a few verses ahead to Revelation 13:3, you will see what happens once chaos begins to break loose on the earth, for then the antichrist will truly be recognized after surviving a fatal wound. Revelation 13:3, (NIV), *"One of the heads of the beast seemed to have had a fatal wound, but the fatal wound had been healed. The whole world will be astonished and follow the beast."*

Review what I have been saying and showing you from the Word of God. It is not the church or the Holy Spirit, rather it is Michael the Archangel, who is the restrainer of evil. If you will ponder these last verses I have just discussed in Revelation 12 and 13, it makes so much sense to me the restrainer of evil has just waged a great battle in the heavens, and satan and his followers have just lost their place in heaven. The Bible says that satan has had a place in heaven where he would go to God and bring accusations against the brethren or against God's people. Now he has just lost his place in heaven. Read Revelation 12:10 (NIV): *"Then I heard a loud voice in heaven say, 'Now have come the salvation and the power and the kingdom of our God and the authority of his Christ. For the accuser of our brothers, who accuses them before our God day and night has been hurled down."*

Is there any doubt who has just restrained the power of wickedness here? It was Michael and the armies of God who have just cast satan to the earth. I can imagine a bit here. Michael has just kicked satan out of the heavens, and he has just won the war God commanded him to fight. Now if you will think about how General Patton and General MacArthur wanted to press on and finish off the enemies of the earth for all time, this is how I imagine Michael would similarly go to the Commander and Chief to seek permission to press on with the battle. I can hear Michael making his appeal to our heavenly Father, "This is our chance, satan and his minions have been pushed back. We have them right where we want them. Just say the word, and I will command your armies to take satan out for all time." Then God replies, "No, Michael, your assignment is completed. I have a different plan for satan. It is now time for you and the armies you command to stand-down." Michael realizes God, in his infinite wisdom, has everything under control. This is where we need to read 2 Thessalonians 2:7-8a (NIV): *"For the secret power of lawlessness is already at work, but the one who now holds it back will continue to do so till he is taken out of the way. And then the lawless one will be revealed."* If you will read this verse carefully, you will see it says the antichrist will not be revealed until the restrainer is taken out of the way.

Now, when you think about this and about what we just covered in the Book of Revelation, chapters 12 and 13, it is just a few verses after satan is thrown down to the earth that a world leader is fatally wounded and then comes back from the dead as the antichrist! It makes sense to me that once satan is thrown down to the earth, this will be the point when the restrainer will be removed.

You may have to be like the Bereans and read and study the Bible verses I have outlined, but what I have presented in this study is very compelling.

2. God has not appointed us to wrath

There are two good verses in the Bible that support the teaching that God has not appointed us to suffer the wrath of God that will take place during the Great Tribulation. The first is found in 1 Thessalonians 5:9 (NIV): *"For God did not appoint us to suffer wrath but to receive salvation through our Lord, Jesus Christ."* The second is found in 1 Thessalonians 1:10 (NIV): *"And to wait for his Son from heaven, whom he raised from the dead - Jesus, Who rescues us from the coming wrath."* From the pre-Tribulation rapture viewpoint, these verses indicate the rapture is a pre-Tribulation event to spare the church from the coming wrath during the Great Tribulation.

Consider that the Bible calls the time-period leading up to his return, "the Great Tribulation", a seven-year time-period that will become more and more intense as Christ's coming approaches. The Bible likens the increase of severe events to birth pains. I believe we are currently entering the time of the birth pains predicted. They could become so severe some Christians may believe the Great Tribulation has started, but if you look at the beginning of the Great Tribulation, with the opening of the seven seals, you will see events that are similar to what has happened for all of time: wars, earthquakes, famine, even the martyrdom of the saints, to which the fifth seal refers. Just as when a woman is getting closer to delivering a child and the intensity of her labor pain increases, that is how it will be when the seals are opened at the beginning of the Great Tribulation. The intensity of war will increase, earthquakes will be more devastating, and famines will be widespread. Most Christians who hold to the pre-Tribulation rapture, believe we will miss out on the seals and all of the Great Tribulation. Many quote 1 Thessalonians 1:10 to try to prove that point. If you look closely at this verse, it says, *"...Jesus who rescues us from the coming wrath."* This means the wrath of God. This verse does not say we will be delivered from tribulation to come. In fact, **think about it, the Great Tribulation is not called the Great Wrath of God**. To me it is obvious the seals are not the wrath of God, for God does not start wars, bring famine, and certainly does not martyr his saints, as described in the fifth seal.

I believe the wrath of God does not start until Revelation 8 and 9 and then picks up again in chapter 15. On the other hand, let us consider what the Bible teaches about tribulation. The Bible says that tribulation "worketh patience". During the Great Tribulation, what is interesting is during the time the saints are battling with the antichrist, God's word says in Revelation 13:10 (NIV): *"...if anyone is to go into captivity, into captivity he will go, if anyone is to be killed with the sword, he will be killed. This calls for patient endurance on the part of the saints."* I believe the Bible is teaching that the saints will be going through a period of tribulation that will bring about the purification of the body of Christ.

Does not the Bible teach us that Christ is coming back for a pure bride, worthy of being called the Bride of Christ? To put this into further Biblical context, read Revelation 13:7-10 (NIV): *"He was given power to make war against the saints and to conquer them. And he was given authority over every tribe, people, language, and nation. All inhabitants of the earth will worship the beast - all whose names have not been written in the book of life belonging to the Lamb that was slain from the creation of the world. He who has an ear, let him hear. If anyone is to go into captivity, into captivity he will go. If anyone is to be killed with the sword, with the sword he will be killed. This calls for patient endurance and faithfulness on the part of the saints."*

These verses are describing some different scenarios believers will be subjected to during the first part of the Great Tribulation. Basically, this is saying for our un-swerving faithfulness and testimony to Christ, that some Christians will be thrown in jail and others will be killed. But we just have to stay true to Christ, knowing they can take our lives but not our eternal souls!

One question I have to ask is, "Does God's Word further support this teaching that the saints will go through a period of tribulation and persecution during this time of the end called the Great Tribulation?" I believe the Bible does give further weight to this thought in 2 Thessalonians 1:4-6, (NIV): *"Therefore among God's churches we boast about your perseverance and faith in all the persecutions and tri-als you are enduring. All this is evidence that God's judg-ment is right, and as a result you will be counted worthy of the kingdom of God, for which you are suffering. God is just; he will pay back trouble to those who trouble you."* As you read further in this chapter, namely verses 7-10a, you will notice the context for this chapter very much concerns the coming of the Lord. These verses are talking about a future time when Christ is revealed and returns to punish those who do not obey the gospel. The passage in 2Thessalonians 1:7-10a (NIV) says, *"And give relief to you who are troubled and to us as well. This will happen when the Lord Jesus is revealed from heaven in blazing fire with his powerful angels. He will punish those who do not know God and do not obey the gospel of our Lord Jesus. They will be punished with everlasting destruction and shut out from the presence of the Lord and from the majesty of his power on the day he comes to be glorified in his holy*

90

people and to be marveled at among all those who have believed. This includes you; because, you believed our testimony to you."

These verses are talking about a time of tribulation the saints will have to endure. These verses are also addressing the church. They clearly say the time-frame for this tribulation and the persecution of the saints will be during the time of the end leading up to the Lord's return.

Earlier in my study, I had mentioned I did not know what the rebellion was. Look at 2 Thessalonians 2:3 in the Kings James Version. You will notice the rebellion is referred to as a great falling away of believers. This is a key point for my position of a mid-Tribulation rapture. I hear so many people say, "What difference will it make whether the rapture is pre-Trib. or mid-Trib. anyway? It will all pan out in the end."

I feel there is a huge difference. What would have happened if Noah had not built the ark or if Joseph had not prepared for the famine in Egypt? How will millions of Christians feel who have been taught Christ is coming to rapture his church away before the Great Tribulation starts, when all of a sudden, the world is thrown into chaos? Imagine if Al Qaeda successfully pulls off their plan that they have had in the works for many years, called the Hiroshima project. The project calls for Al Qaeda terrorists to set off seven or more nukes in seven or more major cities in the United States on the same day. World trade would come to a halt. All the food from store shelves would disappear from panic buying. Most major cities would be overrun with anarchy. All of a sudden we would be thrown into great tribulation. Millions of Christians would question the teachings of their churches, wondering where is the rapture, feeling they had been abandoned by God. I can now see how the stage would be set for a great falling away.

For those who say that God would never leave us to suffer through the Great Tribulation or that God would never abandon us to the torment of the antichrist, my question is, have you ever read <u>Foxe's Book of Martyrs</u>? This book covers centuries of Christians being killed for their unswerving faith in Christ, from the deaths of Christ's disciples, the persecution by the Roman Church in 1200 A.D. to the persecution and killing of Christians that caused them to leave their mother country to come to America for freedom of religion. The author is not talking about water-boarding, as some in our society label as torture. NO! He is talking about Christ's disciple Peter being crucified upside down; because, he did not feel worthy to die the same death as Christ his Lord. He is talking about Christians being beheaded, torn apart by wild beasts, boiled to death, and burned at the stake.

One story that has always stuck in my memory is the story of a Christian who was to be burned at the stake, and he told a friend nearby that he believed God's grace would be sufficient for him to bear up to this death. The friend told him if God's grace is sufficient to raise one finger to let him know. When the flames were engulfing him, he raised up two fingers signifying God's grace was more than enough. When I hear pastors and Christians say God would never abandon his church, I am reminded of Christ's death on the cross when Christ cried out in Matthew 27:46 (KJV): *"And about the ninth hour Jesus cried with a loud voice, saying 'Eli, Eli, Lama Sabachthani.' That is to say, My God, my God, why hast thou forsaken me?"* Did God forsake Jesus Christ his Son? Only in the sense he allowed his Son to die for our sins. If we as Christians have to suffer and die for our faith as martyrs did in ages past, does this mean God has forsaken us? No, because I am reminded of God's promise in Hebrews 13:5b-6 (NIV): *"...because God has said, "Never will I leave you; never will I forsake you.*" *So we say with confidence, 'The Lord is my helper, I will not be afraid. What can man do to me?*"

I believe the first part of the Great Tribulation will be a time of great trials and tribulation that will wake up many in today's Laodicean type church and call all believers to become the pure bride, without spot or wrinkle, for which Christ is coming back. Most importantly, I believe the church will have a major part in the harvest of the lost souls who are not ready for the rapture. To back up this thought, look at the rest of what Revelation has to say about the Laodicean church, namely Revelation 3:19-21 (NIV): *"Those whom I love I rebuke and discipline. So be earnest, and repent. Here I am! I stand at the door and knock. If anyone hears my voice and opens the door, I will come in and eat with him and he with me. To him who overcomes, I will give the right to sit with me on my throne, just as I overcame and sat down with my Father on his throne."* What a thought! Could Jesus be knocking on the door of our churches, calling the backslidden to come back to him with all their heart?

In conclusion, I agree with the pre-Tribulation view that God has not accounted us to the wrath to come. However, I part company with this belief that the seals are the wrath of God. Up until now, I have believed the seals are not part of the wrath of God; because, the fifth seal is the martyrdom of the saints. God would not do this to his own.

Some time ago, I was talking to a pastor friend of mine, and we started talking about the timing of the rapture. When I told him what I had just said, he said he believed the four horses or the first four seals are the wrath of God. Well, the first thing that entered my mind was the first horseman is the revealing of antichrist. Therefore, how could this be the wrath of God? Then the thought hit me regarding the second seal, peace would be taken from the earth. Again, this just does not sound like the wrath of God. Then, looking at the fourth seal, it says in Revelation 6:7-8, (NIV): *"When the Lamb opened the fourth seal, I heard the voice of the fourth living creature say, 'Come!' I looked and there before me was a pale horse, its rider was named Death, and Hades was following close behind him."* This sounds more like the devil, and it sounds like it is coming out of hell and not from God.

Well, I did not express all these thoughts to my pre-Tribulation believing pastor friend. However, as I was driving home, I had a conversation out loud with God, and I kept asking how I might show or explain that the wrath of God does not happen until Revelation 8 with the seven trumpets of God's wrath. I kept asking what is the difference between the seals and the wrath of God. Then it was like this thought just popped into my head. (I believe the Holy Spirit answered my question right there on the spot). **The thought that came to me was, the difference is in the delivery. Angels deliver all of the seven trumpets of God's wrath; angels also deliver the last seven bowls of God's wrath, BUT angels are nowhere involved with the opening of the seals in Revelation 6.** When I arrived home and studied my Bible, all these thoughts were confirmed from God's Word.

A couple of interesting points that go along with this conclusion is about the scroll. Revelation 5:2-3 (NIV): says, *"I saw a mighty angel proclaiming in a loud voice, 'Who is worthy to break the seals and open the scroll?' But no one in heaven or on the earth or under the earth could open the scroll or even look inside it."* **What I notice here is the seals are not <u>in</u> the scroll, they are on the <u>outside</u> of the scroll, and the wrath of God is inside the scroll!**

Also, when you look at the many examples of God's judgment on the nations, you continually see angels involved in

94

the delivery of judgment. There is the angel of death in Egypt and the angels again in Sodom and Gomorrah. Also, there is the angel of the Lord who slew 185,000 Assyrians in one night and the angel who killed thousands in Jerusalem when David took the census against God's wishes. Again I have to say the weight of Scripture is compelling here.

I further believe the rapture is clearly described in Revelation 7, before the wrath of God starts in Revelation 8 and 9. What I will do in the next section of this chapter is show why I believe Revelation 4:1 does not describe the rapture. I will also explain why I believe Revelation 7:9, IS describing the rapture. I think I can show that Scripture leans heavily on the rapture's occurring in the seventh chapter of Revelation.

In closing, I believe we will have to go through some unprecedented times. Yet I am prepared in my heart knowing in whom I have believed and am persuaded that he is able to protect me against that day. Man may hurt my mortal body, but man cannot hurt my eternal soul.

3. Revelation 4:1, the open door to heaven

Revelation 4:1 (NIV): says, *"After this I looked, and there before me was a door standing open in heaven. And the voice I had first heard speaking to me like a trumpet said, 'Come up here, and I will show you what must take place after this."* Then Revelation 4:2 (NIV): says, "At once I was in the Spirit, and there before me was a throne in heaven with someone sitting on it."

These verses from Rev.4:1-2, are interpreted to symbolically represent the rapture of the church. I just do not see the rapture of the church in these verses, I see John, the Revelator, being taken to heaven to the very throne of God,

95

where God told him, "I will show you what must take place after this." If you will go to Revelation 19:11, you will see heaven opened up again just like what happened in Revelation 4:1. Read Revelation 19:11 (NIV): *"I saw heaven standing open, and there before me was a white horse, whose rider is called Faithful and True. With justice he judges and makes war."* This is a revelation of Christ after the battles have been won and the marriage supper of the Lamb is about to take place. This door standing open does not mean a gateway is open for a rapture event, because if you will go back to Revelation 19:6-8, you will discover the saints are already in heaven about to celebrate with Christ at the marriage supper of the Lamb. Read Revelation 19:6-8 (NIV): *"Then I heard what sounded like a great multitude, like the roar of rushing waters, and like loud peals of thunder, shouting:' Hallelujah, for our Lord God Almighty reigns. Let us rejoice and be glad and give him glory, for the wedding of the Lamb has come, and his bride has made herself ready. Fine linen, bright and clean, was given her to wear."*

I would like to know where is a second or third Scripture that shows the timing of the rapture before the Great Tribulation starts. I was taught in Bible school, doctrine has to be backed with the witness of two or three other Scriptures.

Now I will show you a third Scripture verse that shows Paul, in this case, being caught up to heaven to see special revelations from God just like John the Revelator. What Paul experienced does not represent a symbolic rapture of the church either. Read 2 Corinthian 12:3-4 (NIV): *"And I know that this man - whether in the body or apart from the body I do not know, but God knows - was caught up to Paradise. He heard inexpressible things, things that man is not permitted to tell."* Paul's experience is very similar to that which John the Revelator experienced. In fact, in Paul's case, he was "caught up," to Paradise, while John was asked to "Come up here." When the rapture occurs we will not be asked to come up, we will be caught up.

What I see happening here, by those who want to interpret Revelation 4:1 as the rapture of the church is, they are strengthening their position on this doctrine based on the symbolic meaning of what they see in this passage. I believe all doctrine must be supported by the plain speak Word of God, and then let symbolism confirm it. We should not rely on symbolism alone. When you look at Revelation 4:1, it does not say the church is caught up to heaven. In fact, it does not even use the words, 'caught up'. No. Bible scholars have determined there is a symbolic meaning here, and our traditions have accepted it.

I firmly believe we should never interpret Scripture symbolically to establish a doctrinal position. A doctrinal teaching must first be established as literal from the Bible first. Symbolic use of Scripture should only be used to supplement and support what the Bible teaches elsewhere literally, or you can make the Bible say anything you want. This type of interpretation is how cults are established.

What I want to show you is, there are Bible verses that plainly speak of the rapture. I will show you these verses, and then I will show you why Revelation 4:1 does not qualify as a verse that can be used to symbolically support the timing of the rapture. This is very important to understand; because, for someone who holds to the pre-Tribulation view of the rapture, Revelation 4:1 is really the only verse that alludes to the rapture's happening before the Great Tribulation begins. This means the timing of the rapture as a pre-Tribulation event is being established by the use of the symbolic meaning of Revelation 4:1, and that makes for shaky interpretation.

The first verse I will use to show the rapture is, 1 Thessalonians 4:16-17 (NIV): *"For the Lord himself will come down from heaven, with a loud command, with the voice of the archangel and the trumpet call of God, and the dead in Christ will rise first. After that we who are alive and are left will be caught up with them in the clouds to meet the Lord in the air. And so we will be with the Lord forever."* Notice we who are alive are caught up in the clouds to meet the Lord in the air. Next, I will show you other verses that support the Lord's coming in the clouds to meet us at the time of the rapture. Read Matthew 24:30-31 (NIV): *"At that time, the sign of the Son of Man will appear in the sky and all nations of the earth will mourn. They will see the Son of Man coming on the clouds of the sky, with power and great glory. And he will send his angels with a loud trumpet call, and they will gather his elect from the four winds, from one end of the heavens to the other."* Without writing them out, if you look up these other Scripture verses, you will again see the Lord's meeting us in the clouds in Luke 21: 26-27 and Mark 13: 26-27.

Now as you study these verses, it is plain to note that the Lord will come in the clouds, and we are caught up in the clouds to meet the Lord in the air. When you go back and look at Revelation 4:1, John was not caught up in the clouds. In fact, he was not caught up at all. He was told to "Come up here", to the throne of God, just like Paul was brought to the throne.

Another point, John was not caught up at all. Revelation 4:1 (NIV): says, *"...Come up here...."* **When the rapture happens, we are not asked to come up, we are <u>caught up</u>! God does not have to ask or tell us to come; we will be caught up instantly, in the twinkling of an eye.** Another important point is this verse is interpreted to say the church is caught up. How can anyone get church from this verse? This verse does not line up with the literal verses that describe the rapture; therefore, Revelation 4:1 cannot be used to symbolically represent the rapture of the church.

To further show you what I am saying is supported by the Word of God, I will show you that once we are caught up in the clouds, Christ the Son of Man, will lead us to the throne of God. We are not <u>caught up</u> to the throne. I think you will get my point if you will read the vision of Daniel. In Daniel 7:13 (NIV): it says, *"In my vision at night, I looked, and there before me was one like the son of man, coming with the clouds of heaven. He approached the Ancient of Days and was led into his presence."* As you study the rest of Daniel 7, you will see that the saints are released from the grasp of the antichrist and are given the Kingdom. This time when the saints are allowed to possess the Kingdom is the same time as the rapture; because, it goes on to say that the amount of time the antichrist was making war on the saints was three and one half years. This shows the rapture taking place in the middle of the Great Tribulation. Read Daniel 7:21-22 (NIV): ***"As I watched, this horn was waging war against the saints and defeating them, until the Ancient of Days came and pronounced judgment in favor of the saints of the Most High, and the time came when they possessed the kingdom."*** Next, read Daniel 7:25, (NIV). "He will speak against the Most High and oppress his saints and try to change the set times and the laws. **The saints will be handed over to him for a time, times and half a time." (Or three and one half years.)**

What I am saying is, the Bible supports a rapture that does not take place until Revelation 7. You might question where I see two or more Scripture passages to support the rapture occurring after the opening of the six seals in Revelation chapter 6. I will show you several verses in the Bible that show the rapture happening after the opening of the seals during the Great Tribulation. First, I want to show you three places from the Gospels that describe almost verbatim what is happening in the opening of the seals of Revelation, chapter 6. All three describe what I believe to be the rapture happening after the opening of the sixth seal.

I refer you to the following verses:

Matthew 24:4-5 (NIV): *"Jesus answered, "Watch out that no one deceives you. For many will come in my name claiming, 'I am the Christ', and will deceive many...."* This verse coincides with the first seal about false Christs.

Matthew 24:7 (NIV): *"Nation will rise against nation and kingdom against kingdom."* This coincides with the second seal.

Matthew 24:7 (NIV): *"There will be famines and earthquakes in various places."* This coincides with the third seal.

Matthew 24:9 (NIV): *"Then you will be handed over to be persecuted and put to death, and you will be hated of all nations because of me."* This coincides with the fifth seal.

Matthew 24:29 (NIV*): "The sun will be darkened, and the moon will not give its light, the stars will fall from the sky and the heavenly bodies will be shaken."* This coincides with the sixth seal.

Now read Matthew 24: 30-31 (NIV): *"At that time, the sign of the Son of Man will appear in the sky and all the nations of the earth will mourn. They will see the Son of Man coming on the clouds of the sky, with power and great glory, and he will send his angels with a loud trumpet call, and they will gather his elect from the four winds, from one end of the heavens to the other."*

To me, this very clearly describes the events described in Revelation 6. Here you see the opening of the seals; leading up to what I consider the rapture of the believers in Revelation 7:9. Before looking more closely at Revelation 7 to understand where I see the rapture of the believers, let us finish looking at Scriptures that are found in the other gospels that describe the same sequence of events leading up to the rapture that we just read about in Matthew 24.

First, we will look at what the Gospels of Mark and Luke have to say about the rapture and its timing. I will not write out all the passages, but as you read these chapters, you will understand it is talking about a time of Great Tribulation. There are signs that need to happen before the coming of the Lord and culminating with the Lord's coming in the clouds. Read Mark 13:19-27 (NIV): *"Because those will be days of distress unequaled from the beginning, when God created the world, until now and never to be equaled again. If the Lord had not cut short those days, no one would survive. But for the sake of the elect, whom he has chosen, he has shortened them. At that time, if anyone says to you, 'Look, here is the Christ!' Or 'Look, there he is!' Do not believe it. For false Christs and false prophets will appear and perform signs and miracles to deceive the elect, if that were possible. So be on your guard; I have told you everything ahead of time. But in those days, following that distress, the sun will be darkened, and the moon will not give its light, the stars will fall from the sky and the heavenly bodies will be shaken. At that time, men will see the Son of Man coming in the clouds with great power and glory. And he will send his angels and gather his elect from the four winds, from the ends of the earth to the ends of the heavens."*

It is very clear to me that these verses, in the book of Mark, are talking about the rapture, and it is the saints, called the elect, who are being raptured. These are not tribulation saints; because, they are referred to as the elect of God. Think about this, if these spoken about here are the elect of God, then they have to be part of the bride of Christ. If these were tribulation saints, you would have to say that there are two raptures; because, unless the tribulation saints get raptured, they will miss-out on the marriage supper of the Lamb. The Bible does not teach a second rapture for those who are left behind.

If you will read the description of the events that are taking place as described in the gospels you will see it is the same as is described in the sixth seal in Revelation 6:12-13 (NIV): *"I watched as he opened the sixth seal. There was a great earthquake. The sun turned black like sackcloth made of goat's hair, the whole moon turned blood red, and the stars in the sky fell to the earth, as late figs drop from a fig tree when it is shaken by a strong wind."*

Now let us look at Luke 21. This chapter almost completely covers the time of the Great Tribulation. What is interesting is, it is covering both events that are pertinent to the Jews while talking about the events leading up to the saints' rapture at the Lord's return in the clouds. I will pick out three segments that are pertinent to this discussion, and you can study further to verify that I am keeping these verses in their proper context.

Read Luke 21:10-11(NIV): *"Then he said unto them, "Nation will rise against nation and kingdom against kingdom. There will be great earthquakes, famines and pestilences in various places, and fearful events and great signs from heaven...".* Continue on and read Luke 21:16-17 NIV): *"You will be betrayed by parents, brothers, relatives and friends, and they will put some of you to death. All men will hate you because of me. But not a hair of your head will perish. By standing firm you will save yourselves."*

Next examine Luke 21:25-28 (NIV): *"There will be signs in the sun, moon, and stars. On the earth, nations will be in anguish and perplexity at the roaring of the sea. Men will faint from terror, apprehensive of what is coming on the world, for the heavenly bodies will be shaken. At that time, they will see the Son of Man coming in a cloud with power and great glory. When these things begin to take place, stand up and lift up your heads; because, your redemption is drawing near."*

This chapter covers all the seals of Revelation 6. Yet it does not describe the rapture; but it says when these things begin to take place, we are to stand up and lift up our heads, for our redemption is drawing near. When these things happen, why would we want to look up? It is because the Lord's return will be so imminent we will want to be looking heavenward, expecting the Lord to come in the clouds very soon. Also note, the Son of Man is seen coming in the clouds. This is commonly connected with the rapture.

Now let us look at what is happening in Revelation 7, (what I call the rapture of the saints). I believe it is a reasonable interpretation to consider the following as the rapture instead of Revelation 4:1. Start reading Revelation 7:9-12, (NIV): *"After this, I looked, and there before me was a great multitude that no one could count, from every nation, tribe, people and language, standing before the throne and in front of the Lamb. They were wearing white robes and holding palm branches in their hands. And they cried out in a loud voice: 'Salvation belongs to our God, Who sits on the throne and to the Lamb.' All the angels were standing around the throne and around the elders and the four living creatures. They fell down on their faces before the throne and worshiped God saying, 'Amen, praise and glory and wisdom and thanks and honor and power and strength be to our God forever and ever Amen!'"*

Look at verse 9. It says, *"A great multitude from every nation, tribe, language, and people were standing before the throne."* Now go down to verse 13 and hear what one of the elders standing there was saying about this: *"Then one of the elders asked me. These in white robes, who are they? And where did they come from?"*

Imagine this picture. One of the elders, who day and night is around the throne of God, suddenly notices millions, uncountable Christians standing around the throne worshiping God, and he did not know from where they came! See the answer in Revelation 7:14 (NIV): *"I answered, 'Sir, you know', and he said, 'These are they who have come out of the Great Tribulation. They have washed their robes, and made them white in the blood of the Lamb."*

We know these are Christians because their robes have been washed in the blood of the Lamb. My question is, "If these uncountable millions just showed up in heaven after the sixth seal but the rapture happened in Revelation 4:1 before the Great Tribulation started, then who are these who just showed up? Is there a second rapture for the Tribulation saints? I do not see that as Scriptural. To me, what we are seeing here is the church going through part of the Great Tribulation until it gets to the part where the 144,000 Jews are sealed to be God's chosen messengers. They are commissioned to preach and reveal the Love of Christ to the Jewish nation.

At one point I believed this looked like the end of the day of the Gentiles and the start of God's plan to reach out to the children of Israel! I now believe there will be a period of overlap between the end of the day of the Gentiles and the time of reaching out to the Jews. I believe God is already working to lead the Nation of Israel to Christ in time for the rapture, as they are to become an important part of Christ's bride.

104

One argument I have heard against what I have said here is, this is a second rapture, which is for the Jews. **Why would you have a separate rapture of the Jews when you just had the <u>sealing</u> of the 144,000 Jews to evangelize the Jewish nation?** I believe when the one and only rapture occurs, millions of Christian Jews will go up in this rapture; otherwise, they would not be part of the bride of Christ. Furthermore, the two witnesses, who play a part in this, are not even mentioned yet. They are to witness to the Jewish nation for three and one-half years. Also, if you will look at Revelation 7:9, it says these people who have just appeared in heaven came from every nation, tribe, people, and language. The same argument is used here: these are Jews who are living in every nation and speak in every language, but this verse speaks about every <u>people</u>, tribe, nation and language. This verse ties into another verse, which makes for a great deal of excitement. Look at Revelation 5:9 (NIV). This is where only Jesus was qualified to open the seals, and it says, *"You are worthy to take the scroll and to open its seals; because, you were slain and with your blood you purchased men for God from every tribe and language and people and nation."* THIS IS YOU AND ME ABOUT WHOM IT IS TALKING! THIS IS THE CHURCH THAT CHRIST REDEEMED WITH HIS BLOOD. Now look at Revelation 7:9 (NIV), and you will see Christ gathering in the rapture what he has already purchased with his blood! *"After this, I looked and there before me was a great multitude no one could count, from every nation, tribe, people and language."*

Here is where I hope you will pay close attention to what I am going to suggest. I want to take you back to an event between Revelation 4:1 and Revelation 7:11-14. Remember, Revelation 4:1 is the accepted verse for the time of the rapture. Now, look at Revelation 5:11-12 (NIV): *"And behold, and I heard the voice of many angels around the*

105

throne and the beasts and the elders: and the number of them was ten thousand times ten thousand and thousands of thousands, saying with a loud voice, 'Worthy is the Lamb that was slain to receive power and riches and wisdom and strength, and honor and glory and blessing." Notice the persons depicted around the throne-- angels, beasts, and elders. There is no mention of saints around the throne. If the church were raptured in Revelation 4:1, then the saints would be around the throne in white robes in Revelation 5. Also, when you read Revelation 7:11-14, notice the elder who is always around the throne and he asks, "Who are these in white robes...", who have suddenly shown up? The elder answers his own question and says, they are the saints who have come out of the Great Tribulation. **If the rapture had already happened pre-Tribulation in Revelation 4:1,** then the millions of pre-Tribulation Christians would have been in white robes around the throne in both Revelation 5 and 7. **They would have blended in with the multitude about which the elder was asking about in Revelation 7:11-14.** Now do you still think there are two raptures? These verses plainly show the rapture simply could not have happened in Revelation 4:1.

Next, go to 1 Thessalonians 4:15-18. This Scripture shows why the rapture could not have happened until after Revelation 5:11-12(NIV): *"For this we say unto you by the word of the Lord, that we which are alive and remain unto the coming of the Lord shall not prevent them which are asleep. For the Lord himself shall descend from heaven with a shout, with the voice of the archangel, and with the trump of God: and the dead will rise first. Then we which are alive and remain shall be caught up together with them in the clouds, to meet the Lord in the air, and so shall we ever be with the Lord, wherefore comfort one another with these words."*

This Scripture shows why the rapture could not have happened until after Revelation 5:11-12. Read, 1 Thessalonians 4:17 (NIV). It says both the dead in Christ and those who are alive will both be raptured together to meet the Lord, and says further, *"...And so will we be with the Lord forever."* If from the time of the rapture, we will forever be with the Lord, think about it, we would be with the Lord in Revelation 5:11-12 around the throne. If there is no mention of saints in white robes around the throne in Revelation 5:11-12, then the rapture has not yet happened. However, when the elder in Revelation 7: 9-14 asks, *"Who are these multitudes in white robes, **which no man can number?"**,* he answers himself by saying, *"These are they who have come out of the Great Tribulation."* On the other hand, **those in Revelation 5:11-12 ARE numbered!** Can it be any clearer? The rapture, the only rapture, has just taken place in Revelation 7:11-14.

Another argument says that those who have suddenly appeared around the throne in Revelation 7:9 are the martyred saints. However, based on the reaction of the elder, what happened here happened suddenly! The fact that the elder asking the question is always at the throne proves it. It is as if he blinked, and all of a sudden, there are millions in white robes around the throne. This would mean if they were Great Tribulation martyred saints, they would have had to have been killed at the same time. I do not think this is possible. Remember, it says the number of them could not be numbered! In Revelation 5:11, when angelic beings were worshiping around the throne, the numbers were in the millions, but when those in white robes appear, it says in Revelation 7:9 (NIV): *"After this I looked and there before me was a great multitude that no one could count."*

There is a second problem with the above interpretation. When the saints are being martyred, as described in the fifth seal in Revelation 6:9-10, it says the martyred saints are <u>under</u> the altar, not "...at the throne". And they are asking, *"How long until you avenge our blood"?* Then it says they were each given white robes. Now they are still <u>under</u> the altar, not at the throne. If these martyred saints were at the throne in Revelation 6:10 in the white robes given to them while <u>under</u> the altar, the elder in Revelation 7 would not have even noticed a second multitude showing up, for over the last two thousand years, millions of Christians have been martyred. At the rapture, they would all have been at the throne. **Now think about this: if all the martyred saints of all time do not show up at the throne until Revelation 7, how can anyone say the rapture happened in Revelation 4:1?**

When you look at what I have covered concerning whether or not Revelation 4:1 concerns the rapture, the lion's share of Scripture proves this interpretation to be very weak.

4. The church is not mentioned after Rev. 4:1

The fourth argument for the pre-Tribulation position of the rapture concerns the word "church". Because the word church is not mentioned after Revelation 4:1, it is taught that the church was raptured and is no longer on the earth.

My first response to this argument is that this is untrue. The Scriptures say the saints would be martyred during the fifth seal of the Great Tribulation in Revelation 6. Then again, in Revelation 14:11-13, the Bible talks of those who are taking the mark of the beast and the needed patience of the saints during this time. It goes on to say many saints will be martyred at this time. Now I know there are some who teach those saints are tribulation saints. Tell me, where are the words, "Tribulation saints", in the Bible? Plus, realize we are setting the time of the rapture as pre-Tribulation not based on Scripture verses but based on the omission of 'church' after Revelation 4:1. Not only are we basing the timing of the rapture on the omission of 'church', but we are interpreting Revelation 4:1 with a symbolic meaning to make it mean what it has to mean to support a pre-Tribulation rapture.

As I see it, the timing of the rapture is too important to establish this doctrine without Scripture, chapter and verse in plain speak to back it up. Plus, think about this, what is the church? It is the saints that make the church, so if the saints are mentioned after Revelation chapter 4:1, then the church is mentioned. Furthermore, if you study Daniel's vision found in Daniel 7, you will see he speaks about the rapture of the saints taking place in his vision, and there is no mention of the church. It only talks about the saints. I will go into greater detail about the rapture teaching found in Daniel at the end of this chapter.

Another point I would like to make concerning the argument that there is no mention of the church after Revelation 4:1 is, in order for this statement to be accurate, it would have to be true for the whole Bible and not just the book of Revelation. If the CHURCH is mentioned in any other book of the Bible in reference to the church going through the Great Tribulation, then this argument does not hold up. I believe 2 Thessalonians shows the church going through the Great Tribulation, and it is plainly worded without drawing a conclusion based on symbolism.

Read 2 Thessalonians 1:4-10 (NIV): *"Therefore, among God's CHURCHES, we boast about your perseverance and faith in all the persecutions and trials you are enduring. All this is evidence that God's judgment is right, and as a result you will be counted worthy of the kingdom of God, for which you are suffering. God is just: He will pay back trouble to those who trouble you and give relief to you who are troubled, and to us as well. This will happen when the*

109

Lord Jesus is revealed from heaven in blazing fire with his powerful angels. He will punish those who do not know God and do not obey the gospel of our Lord Jesus. They will be punished with everlasting destruction and shut out from the presence of the Lord and from the majesty of his power on the day he comes to be glorified in his holy people and to be marveled at among all those who have believed. This includes you because you believed our testimony to you."

If you will continue reading 2 Thessalonians 2, you will see it is undeniable these chapters concern the time of the Great Tribulation leading up to the Lord's return, the time when Christ returns to put down all evil. Chapter 2 continues to make reference to the time of the antichrist, and 2 Thessalonians 2:1-3 specifically refers to the gathering to Christ, or the rapture, as not occurring until some point after the antichrist arrives.

If this is where I were to stop and say, it is not a strong argument for a pre-Tribulation rapture just because the church is not mentioned after Revelation 4:1, I would have been content. Many times during this study, I have felt the Holy Spirit prompting me to look deeper into His Word through what I would call spontaneous promptings of the Holy Spirit. What I have to share now comes from one of those promptings. I only say this because I know I could not have written this book without the help of the Holy Spirit, and I will not take credit that belongs to God.

I was prompted to study all references concerning the rapture of the church, with the thought that the Bible does not teach Christ is coming back for the church. My first thought was, "Could it be the Bible does not teach Christ is coming back for the church?" With that thought in mind, I opened my Strong's concordance and looked up every reference to church in the Bible. The church is mentioned

110

eighty times, I looked up saints, and saints are mentioned ninety-six times. What immediately jumped out at me was, there is not one single mention of Christ coming back for the church.

There is no mention of the church in heaven, and in fact if you will read the following verses, you will see it is the saints for which Christ is coming back, and it is the saints that will rule with Christ in the ages to come.

Daniel 7:18 (NIV): *"But the saints of the Most High will receive the kingdom and will possess it forever – yes, forever and forever."*

Zechariah 14:5 (KJV): *"....and the Lord my God shall come, and all the saints with thee."*

1Corinthians 6:2 (NIV): *"Do you not know that the saints will judge the world...."*

1 Thessalonians 3:13 (KJV): *"....at the coming of our Lord Jesus Christ with all his saints."*

Jude 14 (KJV): *"And Enoch also the seventh from Adam, prophesied of these, saying, Behold the Lord cometh with ten thousands of his saints."*

In order to get a good handle on what I discovered, I had to ask myself, "Who or what is the church?" It is a given the church is not a building. A building only provides the saints a place to come together to worship and serve God.

So who are these who come together to make up the church? I call them the collection of all those who identify themselves as Christians, as children of God or believers. **We must realize not everyone who calls himself a Chris-**

111

tian is or will be saved. The Bible says even satan believes in God, and we know he will not have a home in heaven.

Read Revelation 2 and 3 about the seven churches of Revelation. It is interesting none of the churches were perfect. Some were better than others but without exception each description of the churches ended with the statement, **"To him who overcomes would receive a reward." This leads me to say that Christ is not coming back for the church but for the over-comer. How does God's Word describe who the over-comers are? They are referred to as the saints or the elect.**

So, when it is noted that the word church is not mentioned after Revelation 4:1, causing the statement to be made that the church was raptured. This is not the case! There is not a single mention in the Bible that Christ is coming back for the church. No, Christ is coming back for his elect, the saints. The fact that the church is not mentioned after Revelation 4:1 is irrelevant. I believe it makes more sense to say the church age is over after Revelation 4:1, for nowhere in God's word does it describe the church going to heaven. No, only individual children of God will go to heaven, and those children are the saints.

In closing, the saints are mentioned after Revelation 4:1; because, the rapture has not yet happened. In fact, the rapture is described in both Revelation 7 and 14, and the saints are mentioned in the context of this event. In the last section of this chapter, from a study in Daniel, I will show how God's Word clearly describes the rapture, this most important event, happening in the middle of the Great Tribulation.

Part two:
Six events that must take place before the Rapture can occur.

Along with the teaching of a pre-Tribulation rapture has been the teaching of the imminent return of the Lord in the rapture. As I show in chapter 6 on what other teachers are teaching concerning the rapture, some teachers have taught that the timing of the rapture has been imminent for almost two thousand years. I was discussing this point with one pastor friend and told him, "How could the rapture have been imminent for even one hundred years if Israel had not been reborn as a nation until 1948?" His response was, "Well, now it is imminent."

When I started this study, there was one verse that convinced me that the rapture was not an imminent event. Now after over three years of working on this study, I believe with the help of the Holy Spirit, I now see that from the time of the rebirth of Israel, (the event that triggers the beginning of the last generation before the return of the Lord Jesus), there are at least seven events that must happen before the rapture of the believers. Only one of these scriptural supported events has been fulfilled. That is the rebirth of Israel in 1948. You may want to go back and review this study concerning the rebirth of Israel in 1948 from my book's introduction. Below, I will go over the remaining six events that must take place before the rapture can occur.

1. The antichrist must be revealed.
2. There must be a falling away

The first two of these six events is plainly shown in God's Word. Realize as you read this, this is not my opinion, this is the Word of God.

2Thessalonians 2:1-3 (NIV): *"Concerning the coming of our Lord Jesus Christ and our being gathered to him, we ask you, brothers, not to become easily unsettled or alarmed by some prophecy, report or letter supposed to have come from us, saying that the day of the Lord has already come. Don't let anyone deceive you in any way, for that day will not come until the rebellion occurs and the man of lawlessness is revealed, the man doomed to destruction."*

These verses are talking about the man of lawlessness, who is the son of perdition or called the antichrist, who must come before the day of the Lord or the rapture occurs. These verses also talk about the rebellion; this is referred to in other translations as a great falling away. I expound further on this falling away throughout my book.

3. The One World Government must be in place before the rapture can occur.

To avoid redundancy, I must encourage you to review chapter 7, "The Coming Antichrist". This chapter clearly shows from God's Word that before the antichrist can be revealed, the ten leaders, or as I call them, "the ten heads of state", and the One World Government must be in place before the rapture can occur. (The antichrist cannot arrive until the One World Government is in place.)Then when you connect this to the first event I have listed above showing that the antichrist must be revealed before the rapture can occur, you start to see a sequence of events that must come together before the rapture can occur.

4. Heavenly events must also take place before the rapture can occur.

This is another instance that is best to let God's Word speak for itself.

Matthew 24:29-31 (NIV): *"Immediately after the distress of those days 'the sun will be darkened, and the moon will not give its light; the stars will fall from the sky, and the heavenly bodies will be shaken. At that time the sign of the Son of Man will appear in the sky, and all the nations of the earth will mourn. They will see the Son of Man coming on the clouds of the sky, with power and great glory. And he will send his angels with a loud trumpet call, and they will gather his elect from the four winds, from one end of the heavens to the other."*

Then read Revelation 6:12-13 (NIV): *"I watched as he opened the sixth seal. There was a great earthquake. The sun turned black like sackcloth made of goat hair, the whole moon turned blood red, and the stars in the sky fell to the earth, as late figs drop from a fig tree when it is shaken by a strong wind."*

As you read both of these verses above, they both refer to the stars falling from the sky. These would be meteor showers. The reference in Revelation 6, places this event at the sixth seal, and the reference from Matthew 24 shows the rapture happening after this event.

5. The temple must be rebuilt before the rapture can occur.

6. The antichrist must desecrate the temple before the rapture can occur.

The following Scriptures will show that both the temple must be rebuilt, and the antichrist must desecrate the temple before the prophecy of these verses can come to pass. The Bible covers both of these events together.

Mark 13:14, 26, 27 (NIV): *"When you see the 'the abomination that causes desolation standing where it does not belong--let the reader understand--then let those who are in Judea flee to the mountains."* Vs 26, *"At that time men will see the Son of Man coming in the clouds with great glory."* Vs. 27, *"And he will send his angels and gather his elect from the four winds, from the ends of the earth to the ends of the heavens."* These verses refer to the antichrist standing in the temple in vs.14, then verse 27, shows the rapture following this event.

To give a second witness to God's own words, you should read Matthew 24:15, 30, *"So when you see standing in the holy place 'the abomination that causes desolation,' spoken of through the Prophet Daniel—let the reader understand'..."*, *"At that time the sign of the Son of Man will appear in the sky, and all the nations of the earth will mourn. They will see the Son of Man coming on the clouds of the sky, with power and great glory."*

These verses show that the rapture cannot happen until the temple is rebuilt; because, how can the antichrist stand in a temple and desecrate a temple that has not yet been rebuilt? If you will look up Daniel 9:27, you will see the timing of this desecration of the temple. A more detailed explanation of this is found in chapter 13 called "a possible scenario story leading up to the rapture", under the subtitle of "2017".

Notice all six of these last remaining events occur during a time period that is recognized as happening during the Great Tribulation. When these events that I have just outlined come to pass it will be the time for us to look up and listen as God admonishes us. Luke 21:28 (NIV): *"When these things begin to take place, stand up and lift up your heads, because your redemption is drawing near."* Truly the last thing that will happen before the Lord returns will be the blowing of the Trumpet, or the last trumpet as is referred to in 1Corinthians 15:52 (NIV*): "In a flash, in the twinkling of an eye, at the last trumpet. For the trumpet will sound, the dead will be raised imperishable, and we will be changed."*

If you will jump ahead to the next chapter, on page 128, I have done a study on the Last Trumpet that I believe you will find quite interesting.

Part three:
Timing of the Rapture from the Book of Daniel.

In chapter 7, I presented information about the coming of the antichrist. Upon further study, I have found more evidence the rapture does not happen until the middle of the Great Tribulation. In the first half of Daniel 7, we have the vision of Daniel described and then explained in the second half. I will show parallel links in the New Testament that show the same events. Then I will end up showing you Daniel's vision not only contains information on the antichrist's war against the saints, but it also shows the deliverance of the saints in the rapture. Then I will take you on a further study of Daniel that shows beyond all doubt that the

117

rapture will be a mid-Tribulation event. Please maintain an open mind as you proceed in this study. Many people who are reading this cannot believe they have never seen what I am showing plainly written in God's Word.

First, let us read the end of Daniel's vision found in Daniel 7:13-14 (NIV): *"In my vision at night I looked, and there before me was one like a son of man, coming with the clouds of heaven. He approached the Ancient of Days and was led into his presence. He was given authority, glory, and sovereign power; all peoples, nations and men of every language worshiped him. His dominion is an everlasting dominion that will not pass away, and his kingdom is one that will never be destroyed."*

When you read this, you will recognize that Jesus is the one who is coming in the clouds. Jesus is coming in the clouds to deliver the saints from the persecution of the antichrist and take them to his Father's kingdom. Looking further at this verse, you will see it is addressing the Gentiles, not the Jews, as this event is the rapture of the saints out of all nations of the world. Read Daniel 7:14a (NIV): *"He was given authority, glory, and sovereign power; all peoples, nations and men of every language worshiped him."* My point will become even clearer as the meaning of Daniel's visions and dreams are explained in the second half of Daniel 7. Read Daniel 7:21-22, (NIV): *"As I watched, this horn was waging war against the saints and defeating them, until the Ancient of Days came and pronounced judgment in favor of the saints of the Most High, and the time came when they possessed the kingdom."* I believe "kingdom" is referring to the kingdom of heaven. For the saints to possess the kingdom of heaven, they have to go to heaven.

I want to show you the parallel of Jesus coming in the clouds for his saints from Matthew 24:29-31 (NIV): *"Immediately after the distress of those days, 'the sun will be*

118

darkened, and the moon will not give its light; the stars will fall from the sky, and the heavenly bodies will be shaken.' At that time the sign of the Son of Man will appear in the sky, and all nations of the earth will mourn. They will see the Son of Man coming on the clouds of the sky, with power and great glory. And he will send his angels with a loud trumpet call, and they will gather his elect from the four winds and from one end of the heavens to the other."

These verses from Matthew are almost verbatim of those in Mark 13:24-27, and Acts 2:20 (NIV): *"The sun will be turned to darkness and the moon to blood before the coming of the great and glorious day of the Lord."* These events are also seen in the sixth chapter of Revelation, with the opening of the seals. Notice the fifth seal is the martyrdom of the saints, parallel to what is happening in Daniel described as war on the saints.

Please stay with me, for it is about to get very interesting. For now, I will further link these Scriptures to the Book of Revelation and Acts. Read Revelation 6:12-13 (NIV): *"I watched as he opened the sixth seal. There was a great earthquake. The sun turned black like sack cloth made of goat hair, the whole moon turned blood red, and the stars in the sky fell to the earth, as late figs drop from a fig tree when shaken by a strong wind."* What is spoken of in Revelation 6:12-13 is the fulfillment of that which Acts 2:20 says must happen before the day of the Lord comes. Acts 2:20, (NIV): *"The sun will be turned into darkness and the moon to blood before the coming of the great and glorious day of the Lord."* Some may ask, "Is the rapture the day of the Lord?" If you will read 2Peter3:10 (NIV), it throws light on this, *"But the day of the Lord will come like a thief."*

Now I will show you the arrival of the saints in heaven as described in Daniel 7:13 and Revelation 7:9. First, read

119

Daniel 7:13,14a (NIV): *"In my vision at night, I looked, and there before me was one like a son of man, coming with the clouds of heaven. He approached the Ancient of Days and was led into his presence. He was given authority, glory and sovereign power; all peoples, nations and men of every language worshiped him."*

Now read Revelation 7:9 (NIV): *"After this I looked and there before me was a great multitude that no one could count, from every nation, tribe, people, and language, standing before the throne and in front of the Lamb. They were wearing white robes and were holding palm branches in their hands."*

To bring these thoughts to their conclusion, I want to share the meaning of Daniel's vision that was given to him in the second half of Daniel 7. First, I want to show the verse in Daniel that shows the antichrist waging war against the saints until God steps in and delivers the saints. This deliverance is the rapture that is described as the Son of Man coming in the clouds in Daniel 7:13 and then shown in greater detail in Matthew 24:29-31. Next read Daniel 7:21 (NIV*): "As I watched, this horn was waging war against the saints and defeating them, until the Ancient of Days came and pronounced judgment in favor of the saints of the Most High, and the time came when they possessed the kingdom."* What is interesting is this oppression or war against the saints has an ending point described in this verse above. It says the horn is waging war against the saints and defeating them until the Ancient of Days steps in to deliver them.

In reading the next verse, you will see how long the saints must endure the oppression from the antichrist. Read Daniel 7:25 (NIV): *"He will speak against the Most High and oppress his saints and try to change the set times and the laws. The saints will be handed over to him for a time,*

120

times, and half a time." The margin of my Thompson Study Bible says this time is three and one half years. Now think about this, the antichrist appears on the scene at the opening of the first seal of Revelation 6. The antichrist is not on the earth as the actual antichrist until satan possesses one of the horns or heads of the beast and brings this Head of State back from the dead. Once satan is this world leader in human form, you can be sure he will lash out against the saints almost immediately. Daniel teaches that the antichrist will broker a seven year peace with Israel soon after he comes to power. The Bible supports that this is the beginning of the seven year Great Tribulation. Now, what is interesting is the antichrist will only be able to make war against the saints for three and one half years according to Daniel 7:25. Why will the antichrist no longer be able to make war on the saints? Daniel 7:21-22 shows the reason, **God intervenes!** What is the form of this intervention? **Jesus is coming in the clouds and raptures the saints!** Put these thoughts all together, and you have the rapture occurring three and one half years into the Great Tribulation.

I believe I have shown a strong case for the rapture as a mid-Tribulation event from the Book of Daniel. One question I anticipate is whether the Book of Daniel supports my conclusion elsewhere in the book of Daniel. My answer is a strong YES. I will outline below further Biblical support from the Book of Daniel that shows the rapture as a mid-Tribulation event.

If you read Daniel 12:1-2, you will realize these verses are talking about the time of the Great Tribulation. These verses then describe a deliverance from this time of Great Tribulation. (Notice that Michael the archangel is standing up and ready to play a part in this coming deliverance.) What is the form of this deliverance which is being referred to? If you will notice who are included in this event, you will

121

realize it must be talking about the rapture of the saints. Read Daniel 12:1-2, (NIV): *"At that time Michael the great prince who protects your people, will arise. There will be a time of distress such as has not happened from the beginning of nations until then. But at that time your people – everyone whose name is found written in the book – will be delivered. Multitudes who sleep in the dust of the earth will awake: some to everlasting life, others to shame and everlasting contempt."*

When you see the dead in Christ who have their names written in the Book of Life, awakening from the sleep of death, clearly the event described here is the rapture. Read 1Thessalonians 4:15-18 (NIV): *"According to the Lord's own word, we tell you that we who are still alive, who are left till the coming of the Lord, will certainly not precede those who have fallen asleep. For the Lord himself will come down from heaven, with a loud command, with the voice of the archangel and the trumpet call of God, and the dead in Christ will rise first. After that, we who are still alive and are left will be caught up with them in the clouds to meet the Lord in the air. And so we will be with the Lord forever. Therefore encourage each other with these words."*

This is a WOW moment for me. When you read above where it says, "For the Lord himself will come down from heaven, with a loud command, with the voice of the archangel..." Michael is the archangel, one of the top generals in command of the armies of God, and Daniel 12:1 shows Michael getting ready to play his part in the rapture of all those whose names are written in the Book of Life, who are the elect of God, or the saints.

It is interesting that after these coming events were described in Daniel 12:1-2, it goes on to say in Daniel 12:4, that these words were to be sealed up until the time of the end. Daniel 12:4 (NIV): *"But you, Daniel, close up and seal the words of the scroll until the time of the end..."* If you read further, it gets very interesting, as verses 5-7 describe two men standing on both sides of the river talking to a man in linen that was above them. I believe the man in linen was Jesus and the other two may have been Michael, the archangel (and maybe another angel). One of the men or an angel asks the question, *"How long will it be before these astonishing things are fulfilled?"* What are the astonishing things referred to? The things referred to in Daniel 12:1-2 are the time of the Great Tribulation up until the time of the deliverance of God's people whose names are written in the Book of Life, both the living and those who are dead in the Lord. Then the man in linen – who I believe is Jesus – answers the question and describes this time as *"a time, times, and half a time"*, (or three and one-half years). This places the rapture three and one-half years into the Great Tribulation.

Now read Daniel 12:5-8 and see if what I am saying makes sense.   Daniel 12:5-8 (NIV): *"Then I Daniel, looked, and there before me stood two others, one on this bank of the river and one on the opposite bank. One of them said to the man clothed in linen, who was above the waters of the river, 'How long will it be before these astonishing things are fulfilled?' The man clothed in linen who was above the waters of the river, lifted his right hand and his left hand toward heaven, and I heard him swear by him who lives forever, saying, "It will be for a time, times, and half a time. When the power of the holy people has been finally broken, all these things will be completed."*

Again notice the last part of the answer from the one in linen. It says that once the power of the holy people has been broken, all these things will be completed. Realize that during this time of the Great Tribulation, the antichrist has been waging war against the saints. About this time, the antichrist will enter the temple and declare that he is God.

Now get the picture of what is happening here. Daniel has just had it explained to him how long it would be until these astonishing things would be fulfilled. However, Daniel still does not get the full picture. So again he asks another question. The question is not about the fulfillment of the astonishing things but about the outcome of all of these things. Read Daniel 12:8-11 (NIV): *"I heard, but I did not understand. So I asked, "My Lord, what will the outcome of all this be?"* He replied, "Go your way, Daniel, because the words are closed up and sealed until the time of the end. Many will be purified, made spotless and refined, but the wicked will continue to be wicked. **None of the wicked will understand. From the time that the daily sacrifice is abolished and the abomination that causes desolation is set up, there will be, 1290 days."**

This is another revelation moment for me. Daniel has had two questions answered in Daniel chapter 12. The first question concerned the time when the astonishing things would be fulfilled. He was told it would be three and one-half years to the time that the saints would be delivered coinciding with the antichrist desecrating the temple. Then Daniel asks what the outcome of all this would be. The Kings James Version says, "What shall be the end of these things?" He was told it will be three and one half years from the time that the daily sacrifice is abolished, the same time that the antichrist is desecrating the temple, until all these things will come to their end. The answers to these two questions have established two things: how long from the beginning of the Great Tribulation to the deliverance of the saints (three and one-half years) and how long from the desecrating of the temple until the end of these things, again (three and a half years).I believe God's Word in Daniel

124

12 supports my conclusion that the rapture of the church occurs in the middle of the seven- year Great Tribulation period.

In closing, consider the question that some will ask, "Is it really that important when the Lord returns? Should not we just be ready?" This is a good question. If the church has been taught that the rapture will come before the Great Tribulation starts, this gives the church a false sense of security. I have heard pastors say God would not allow his church to go through suffering. I showed from God's Word previously in Revelation 14:11-13, that the saints will have to have patient endurance during the Great Tribulation. This will also be the time when the antichrist is pushing his system of the mark of the beast.

If the saints, who have expected the pre-Tribulation rapture, all of a sudden realizing they are in the Great Tribulation with no warning to get ready for this turbulent time, I believe it will cause many Christians to turn away from God. They will believe God has abandoned them and that their Christian leaders have misled them. They will then accept the system of the antichrist rather than starve to death. I believe the events happening today with the world economies on the verge of collapse are setting the world stage to make it easy for the world populations to accept a savior in the form of the antichrist.

We, as believers, have to be the ones looking for the signs of Christ's coming. I am convinced we must prepare for hard times as Joseph did, so when the hard times come, we will be able to take care of the needs of our family and others. We need to be in a position for God to use us for the greatest revival the world has ever seen! If what I have written in this chapter makes sense, I urge you to shout it from the housetops, and help spread the message of this book, for the time is short.

9. Post-Tribulation view of the rapture

In my studies, I have read that five to ten percent of Christians believe the rapture will not happen until the end of the Great Tribulation. I was not going to cover this view in my book because I have always believed this position is indefensible. If you keep the integrity of God's Word, I do not believe you can defend a doctrinal position that contradicts other portions of God's Word. God's Word will not contradict itself. When I decided to cover this position, I decided I would pick the two most commonly used Scriptural arguments in favor of the post-Tribulation view and show why this position is flawed. Once I have covered the first argument for the post-Tribulation view, then I will cover the second.

One of the arguments for the post-Tribulation position found in God's Word is in 1 Corinthians 15:52 (NIV): *"In a flash, in the twinkling of an eye, at the last trumpet, for the trumpet will sound, the dead will be raised imperishable, and we will be changed."* Some who hold to the post-Tribulation view will say there is only one last trumpet found in the Bible, which is the last trumpet of the seven trumpets of God's wrath found in the book of Revelation. One problem I see with using this verse for the post-Tribulation position is the last trumpet of the seven trumpets of God's wrath still leaves the seven bowls of God's wrath to come. This would mean the rapture occurs in the middle of God's wrath not at the end of God's wrath.

Furthermore; if you will read the reference in Revelation that has the last trumpet contained in it, Revelation 11:15 (NIV): *"The seventh angel sounded his trumpet, and there were loud voices in heaven which said, 'The kingdom of the world has become the Kingdom of our Lord and of his*

Christ. And he will reign forever and ever," this verse gives no hint of the rapture having just taken place. It sounds like the victory over evil has been won. This does not sound like a rapture verse. If you could say this verse sounds as if the rapture has just taken place, then you would have a serious problem keeping the integrity of God's Word, for as I have said, God's Word will not contradict itself. Take a look at 1 Thessalonians 1:10, and you will find a major contradiction: *"And to wait for his Son from heaven, whom he raised from the dead - Jesus who rescues us from the coming wrath."* Then read 1 Thessalonians 5:9 (NIV): *"For God did not appoint us to suffer wrath but to receive Salvation through our Lord Jesus Christ."*

The Word of God clearly shows we will not be on earth when the wrath of God is happening. If you read these chapters in the Bible which contain the verses I am using, they show we will not experience the wrath of God. You will see both of these chapters are talking about the coming of the Lord and the rapture. Now I know some will say God can protect us in the midst of his wrath, but if you study the wrath of God, you will see vast areas of the earth are destroyed. When the fifth trumpet of God's wrath is delivered, the scorpion creatures are released. It only says they are not to touch the 144,000 sealed Jews who were from the twelve tribes of Israel. **Why is there no provision for the saints to be untouched by the scorpion creatures? It is simple. The saints are not on the earth; they have been raptured before the wrath of God starts.**

I do not believe there is a contradiction in the Word of God that cannot be explained if you study and look for an explanation. If you will look at the alternative explanation concerning the last trumpet that I will be making, I believe you will see this makes a lot of sense.

When the book of 1 Corinthians was written, the book of Revelation did not exist. In fact, it could have been forty more years before the aged Apostle John wrote the book of Revelation. Now I know it could be possible for God to reference a book that is not yet written, but we are dealing with a contradiction that compels us to look for an alternative explanation from God's Word.

A Study of the Last Trumpet

Those who are of the persuasion of a post-Tribulation rapture based on the last trumpet, who say there is only one last trumpet found in the Bible, namely in the book of Revelation, are not entirely correct. Ask yourself, what would someone reading 1 Corinthians 15:52(NIV), when it was first written, have thought this verse was talking about, when it said, *"At the last trumpet, for the trumpet will sound, the dead will be raised imperishable and we will be changed"*? I believe, from a Jewish mindset, they would have thought it referred to the trumpets of the annual Feast of Trumpets celebrated every year. I have done a study on the Feast of Trumpets, and what I found is very interesting.

A significant reference to the Feast of Trumpets is found in Leviticus 23:23-24 (NIV): *"The Lord said to Moses, say to the Israelites; on the first day of the seventh month you are to have a day of rest, a sacred assembly commemorated with trumpet blasts."* This feast occurs on the seventh month of the Jewish calendar. It falls on the new moon, so the exact day is not known, but it is around the last day of the month of September on our calendar. The shofar, or ram's horn, is blown at different times during this event for the purpose of calling the faithful to repentance and consecration. Interestingly, the Feast of Trumpets is one of three religious festivals that fall in the same seventh month. There are a total of seven festivals celebrated throughout the year, and three fall in a one-month period. The first of these three is the Feast of Trumpets followed by the Day of Atonement and culminating with the Feast of Tabernacles.

These festivals are celebrated as a memorial to past events, and the Feast of Trumpets is a remembrance of God's meeting with Moses on Mount Sinai, the account of which is found in Exodus 19. At that time, God gave Moses the Ten Commandments, establishing the covenant of the Old Testament. If you will follow along with me in the text I will share, you will see a special event happened on the third day. It appears this blast of the trumpet on the third day is the important blast which the Jews were awaiting. This being the LAST TRUMPET of this celebration.

To prepare for this event on the third day, they were to wash their clothes. It was to be a time of repentance and consecration. On the third day there was lightning and clouds in the mountain of God, and when the blast of the trumpet went off, Moses was to lead the people to meet God. It appears this biggest of the blasts, was the last and most significant blast of this event. Now read, Exodus 19:13b-17 (NIV): *"Only when the ram's horn sounds a long blast, may they go up to the mountain. After Moses had gone down the mountain to the people, he consecrated them, and they washed their clothes. Then he said to the people, 'Prepare yourselves for the third day, and abstain from sexual relations.' On the morning of the third day, there was thunder and lightning, and a thick cloud formed over the mountain, and a very loud trumpet blast was heard. Everyone in the camp trembled, and then Moses led the people out of the camp to meet with God."*

Think about this: when Christ comes again, we will get new robes washed in the Blood of the Lamb. It was on the third day that Christ rose from the dead, and it appears this is the third day of The Feast of Trumpets. Then when we hear the last trumpet, the dead in Christ will rise first, and we who are alive will be raptured. Instead of Moses leading his people to the mountain of God, Jesus will lead us to the presence of our heavenly Father. Note, that it mentions that a thick cloud formed over the mountain, and when Jesus comes for His Bride, he will be seen coming in the clouds.

When you read Hosea 6:2, (KJV), you see another Old Testament example to this line of thought. *"After two days will he revive us: in the third day he will raise us up, and we shall live in his sight."* Then read, 1 Corinthians 15:52, (NIV), and it all fits together. *"In a flash, in the twinkling of an eye, at the last trumpet, for the trumpet will sound, the dead will be raised imperishable, and we will be changed."*

I see another problem with using the last trumpet of 1 Corinthians for the timing of the rapture. Some teachers call this a mid-Tribulation verse. How can this verse show the mid-Tribulation position, when this verse shows the saints going through six trumpets of God's wrath. How can we be protected from God's wrath and still go through it? A second thought is; if we are going through the wrath of God, "Why have a rapture at all?" I just do not see this verse supporting either the mid or post-Tribulation view.

Another argument used to support the post-Tribulation view is found in Matthew 24:29-31 (NIV): *"Immediately after the distress of those days, the sun will be darkened, and the moon will not give its light; the stars will fall from the sky, and the heavenly bodies will be shaken. At that time, the sign of the Son of Man will appear in the sky, and the nations of the earth will mourn. They will see the Son of Man coming on the clouds of the sky, with power and great glory. And he will send his angels with a loud trumpet call, and they will gather his elect from the four winds, from one end of heavens to the other."*

Those who believe in the post-Tribulation view, take the first statement in these verses, *"immediately after the distress of those days"*, to mean immediately after the end of the seven-year Great Tribulation, when Christ will come for his elect or saints. There are a couple of problems with this interpretation. One is, the seven-year Great Tribulation consists of two major parts. There is the pre-wrath portion to the Great Tribulation, and there is the wrath of God portion. Now I realize some people believe the wrath of God starts with the opening of the seals. I feel I have addressed this adequately, earlier in this study in chapter 8 under the subtitle, "God has not appointed us to wrath." In this previous chapter, it shows why it is reasonable to see why the opening of the seals is not the wrath of God that will start in Revelation 8.

In order to better understand why I do not believe the above argument from the post-Tribulation view is correct, we need to figure out where, in the Great Tribulation, does what is described in these verses in Matthew 24 line up with what is happening during the Great Tribulation. If you will look at the sixth seal of Revelation, you will have to agree we have a match. Read Revelation 6:12-13 (NIV*):* *"I watched as he opened the sixth seal. There was a great earthquake. The sun turned black like sackcloth made of goat hair, the whole moon turned blood red, and the stars in the sky fell to earth, as late figs drop from a fig tree when shaken by a strong wind."* Now compare this with what is said in Matthew 24:29 (NIV): *"...The sun will be darkened, and the moon will not give its light; the stars will fall from the sky, and the heavenly bodies will be shaken."* Consider this: these two different books of the Bible were written years apart by two different writers, yet they are very similar. When read in full context, they are, in fact, describing the same event. To me it just makes sense the rapture will happen after the distress of those days as explained in Revelation, chapter 6--before the wrath of God starts in Revelation, chapter 8.

This brings up another problem. If you believe the rapture is a pre-Tribulation event, Matthew 24:31 looks to be describing the rapture, but the timing is not a pre-Tribulation rapture. Those who hold to the pre-Tribulation view need to come up with an explanation; because, this looks like a mid-Tribulation rapture.

One well known teacher on the rapture and the end-times has come up with such an explanation. I will share his view on this and show why it fails to fit in with the rest of Scripture. In order to explain how this pre-Tribulation teacher handles this problem, read Matthew 24:31 (NIV): *"And he will send his angels with a loud trumpet call, and they will gather his elect from the four winds, from one end of the heavens to the other."*

What this teacher explains is the elect who are being spoken about here are the Jews and not the Christian church. If you do a study on the elect, you will realize God has called many different people his elect, and in fact, a study will show you his angels are his elect, some individuals are his elect, Christians are his elect, and the Jews are his elect. So what you have to determine is to which elect is this verse in Matthew 24:31 referring.

The pre-Tribulation teacher I was watching on television explained that when the book of Matthew was written, the church was not formally started; therefore, this verse is addressing the Jewish audience. So according to him, the elect that are being raptured here are the Jewish remnant survivors of the Great Tribulation. There are a couple of problems with this explanation. The biggest one is when the disciples accepted Christ as their Savior and Messiah, that was the start of the church and they were all Jews during the formation of the early church. I realize some teachers will say the church was not started until Jesus died on the cross. I do not go along with this; because, when Jesus was calling his disciples together, he was not forming a Jewish synagogue. He was teaching a New Covenant and those who were accepting his teaching were the nucleus of the church. The church was open before the cross; Jesus dying on the cross was the grand opening of the church.

When the rapture occurs, both Jews and Gentiles who have accepted Christ will go up to be with our Lord. The Jews who will go through the rest of the Great Tribulation will go through it; because, they did not accept Jesus as their Lord before the rapture happens. Think about this: how can the elect spoken about here be the Jews who would be raptured off the earth at the end of the sixth seal? There would not be any Jews in Israel for Jesus to come back and save at the battle of Armageddon!

In conclusion, this description of the rapture is not describing a post-Tribulation event; because, it happens after the opening of the seals before the wrath of God starts. It is too soon to be the post-Tribulation rapture.

This description of the rapture is not a pre-Tribulation rapture; because, it happens after the opening of the seals. The Great Tribulation is well under way.

It is not the rapture of the Jews; because, they have to be in Israel until the battle of Armageddon, except for those who accept Christ as their Lord. These go up in the same rapture as the saints.

Now, we only have one other choice: these verses are describing the rapture of the believers in the <u>middle</u> of the Great Tribulation.

10. A warning to those who add or subtract from God's Word

The Bible gives a warning to anyone who adds or subtracts from the Word of God and more specifically adding or subtracting from the prophecy of the Book of Revelation. Revelation 22:18-19 (NIV): says, *"I warn everyone who hears the words of the prophecy of this book; if anyone adds anything to them, God will add to him the plagues described in this book. And if anyone takes words away from this book of prophecy, God will take away from him his share in the tree of life and in the holy city, which are described in this book."* I think it is interesting God puts this warning in the Book of Revelation. It is as if God knew man would struggle to get its interpretation right.

There are rules for proper Bible interpretation, and some are so basic they should never be violated. One of these basic rules is to always take the Word of God in its proper context. What this means is when you are taking a Scripture from a book in the Bible, you must look at what is being said before and after the Scripture you are using as your text from which to teach or preach. This helps put it in its proper context.

I will give you an example of how a teacher of the Word of God can be guilty of taking away from the Word of God. Read 1 Thessalonians 5:2-3 (NIV): *"For you know very well that the day of the Lord will come like a thief in the night. While people are saying, 'Peace and safety,' destruction will come on them suddenly, as labor pains on a pregnant woman, and they will not escape."* Now this verse is often used to teach that the rapture will come without warning and we will not know when the Lord is coming. Thus, it is often used to help teach the pre-Tribulation position of the rapture and the imminent return of the Lord. What is wrong with using this verse in this way is key words are omitted to make a point that is not true. If you look at the next two verses, you will see this Scripture is teaching something different. Read 1 Thessalonians 5:4-5 (NIV): *"But you are not in darkness so this day should surprise you like a thief. You are all sons of light and sons of the day. We do not belong to the night or to the darkness."* **By putting these verses in proper context, we learn that those who are living in darkness will be caught like a thief in the night when the Lord returns, but those who are living in the light will not be surprised when the Lord comes back. Those who are in the light should not be caught off-guard. We should be looking for his coming, and when the signs of Christ's coming are happening, it will be time to look up, for the Scripture says, Luke 21:28, "then Look up, and lift up your heads; for your redemption is drawing near !"**

That was an example of taking away from the Word of God. Now I will show a couple of examples of adding to God's Word. I will not mention the name of the preacher, but a well-known international preacher and teacher wrote a book on Revelation. In his book, he misquotes Matthew 24:36 (NIV): *"No one knows about that day or hour, not even the angels in heaven, nor the Son, but only the Father."* When he quotes this verse in his book, he says, "No man knows the day, the hour or the year." What he has done is add the word 'year', and this changes everything. With the Word of God as God wrote it, when the signs of Christ's coming are happening, we will be able to look up and realize the Lord is coming at any time. We can truly expect his soon appearance. But when you add just this one word, 'year', you are supporting the pre-Tribulation view of the rapture by changing the Word of God. This teaching says we will be raptured imminently, without warning.

135

Under the teaching of a mid-Tribulation view of the rapture, the rapture will take place after the six seals of the book of Revelation 6. When these events are happening, the saints will realize it is now the time for Jesus to return, and even though we will not know the day or the hour, we will be able to know Christ is coming any day now.

Read Luke 21:25-28 (NIV): *"There will be signs in the sun, moon and stars. On the earth, nations will be in anguish and perplexity at the roaring and tossing of the sea. Men will faint from terror, apprehensive of what is coming on the world, for heavenly bodies will be shaken. At that time they will see the Son of Man coming in a cloud with power and great glory. When these things begin to take place, stand up and lift up your heads, because your redemption is drawing near."* When the word, 'year', is added, it gives weight to the pre-Tribulation view of the rapture; because, if the rapture happens <u>after</u> the seals, we would know this is the year.

A second example of adding to Gods Word is when we are taught the saints that are being martyred and going through the time of the war on the saints are **tribulation saints**. The title, tribulation saints, is not in the Bible. Again, in order to teach the pre-Tribulation position, you have to explain who these saints are that are going through part of the Great Tribulation. So what has been done is to add, "tribulation" to saints in our teaching, saying that these saints were not ready for the rapture and were left behind to go through the Great Tribulation. Again when you have to add words to God's Word to strengthen your doctrinal position, you are violating Gods command and building your doctrines on a house of cards.

In the book of Daniel, Daniel was told to seal up what he saw until the time of the end. When John the Revelator was writing the Book of Revelation, he heard and saw things he was told not to write down. Now, I do not know what he was told not to write, but it is clear from Daniel some things were not meant to be revealed until the time of the end. Most people say the pre-Tribulation rapture doctrine originated less than two hundred years ago. Some teachers say this teaching goes back to about two hundred years after Christ's death. The truth is the pre-Tribulation doctrine did not receive acceptance until around 1830 when John Darby introduced it.

I believe the doctrine of the pre-Tribulation rapture, in spite of how entrenched it is in our doctrines of faith, emerged because of the impatience of man's, not wanting to wait until the time of the end. With little weight of Scripture to back-up this teaching, we have insisted we can take a round peg and force it into a square hole. I believe the confusion that will arise from the discovery that the church will not be raptured before the seals of Revelation chapter six, will lead to mass confusion in the church. Many believers will fall away and follow after the lies of the antichrist; many will be convince that he is the true God. Read 2 Thessalonians 2:3-4 (KJV): *"Let no man deceive you by any means, for that day shall not come except there come a falling away first, and that man of sin be revealed, the son of perdition; who opposed and exalted himself above all that is called God, or that is worshiped; so that he as God sitteth in the Temple of God, showing himself that he is God."*

When this great confusion comes, who will be to blame? I believe the answer can be found in 2 Peter 3. This whole chapter is relevant to what we are studying about concerning the last days and the coming of the Lord for his believers. There are three sections very relevant to what I am saying here. The first is found in 2 Peter 3:3-4 (NIV): *"Knowing this first, that there shall come in the last days scoffers,*

137

walking after their own lusts, and saying, where is the promise of his coming? For since the fathers fell asleep, all things continue as they were from the beginning of creation." **Think about what this verse is saying. Scoffers are taunting believers by saying, "Where is the promise of his coming?" Why would scoffers be saying this? What makes the most sense to me is, when the Great Tribulation starts and the seals are being opened, and the rapture has not happened, then scoffers and unbelievers will taunt the saints and say, "I thought all you saints were going to disappear and leave us behind, but it appears as if you have been left behind!"**

At this time, Christians will be looking for answers as to why the rapture has not taken place. As you read further in this chapter, the Lord gives us the answer as to why we are to wait and why he has not yet come back for us. Read 2 Peter 3:9 (KJV): *"The Lord is not slack concerning his promise as some men count slackness; but is long-suffering to us-ward, not willing that any should perish, but that all should come to repentance."* Think about what this verse is saying; *"The Lord is not slack concerning his promise..."* If you read this chapter and the verses on both sides of this verse, you will see he is talking about the promise of his return. **Why would men say the Lord is slack concerning his promise? I believe it is because when the rapture does not happen according to OUR interpretation of God's Word, we will be complaining to God and asking him why he has not come to take us out of here?** Then the Lord gives us the answer in this same verse. The Lord goes on to say, **"The Lord is long-suffering to us-ward, not willing that any should perish, but that all should come to repentance." Can it be said any more plainly? The Lord wants to hold off his coming for his bride, the church, or saints until as many as will accept him do and are saved.**

If we are in God's army and we have been given The Great Commission to preach the gospel to the world, then why would God want to take his army home when the greatest opportunity to win the lost will be during this time? I believe the doctrine of the pre-Tribulation rapture that says, "If you are not ready, one of these days you will be left behind" is a doctrine born by the nature of man. That would say, "If you do not accept Christ and live right, you will regret it and be left behind." I believe the nature of God who so loved the world that he gave his only Son so that we could be saved, is a God of grace and love, who is not willing that any should perish--whose wish is that all who will, would come to the knowledge of the truth.

If you will read further in 2 Peter 3, you will see a warning that we need to interpret the Scriptures carefully or we might make some serious mistakes in establishing our belief system. Read 2 Peter 3:16 (KJV): *"As also in all his epistles, speaking in them of things; in which are some things hard to be understood, which they that are unlearned and unstable wrest, as they do also the other scriptures, unto their own destruction."* What I see being explained here is all the epistles or books of the Bible have things that are hard to understand. In this chapter, Peter has been talking of the Lord's return, so its immediate meaning is, it is hard to understand the meaning of the Word of God concerning the coming of the Lord. In short, God is a God of second chances.

Then this verse goes on to say there are those who wrest or interpret the Scriptures unto their own destruction. I believe when the saints realize the rapture is not happening before the tribulation period, it will cause so much confusion it will be a destructive event to the church. It will cause many to believe God has abandoned them, and many will fall away from God as warned in 2 Thessalonians 2:1-3 (KJV): *"Now we beseech you, brethren, by the coming of our Lord*

Jesus Christ, and our gathering together unto him, that ye be not soon troubled, neither by spirit, nor by word, nor by letter as from us, as that the day of the Lord is at hand. Let no man deceive you by any means; for that day shall not come, except there come a falling away first, and that man of sin be revealed, the son of perdition." Can it be said any clearer? The gathering together unto him is talking about the rapture. It plainly says this event will not happen until a falling away happens, an event where many saints turn away from God. Then it says the man of sin, or the antichrist, must first be revealed. This means the rapture cannot happen until the antichrist is revealed. Yet I hear it being taught by ministers of the pre-Tribulation persuasion, if you see the antichrist show up, then you have been left behind.

After recently studying the book of Zechariah, much of which concerns the Second Coming of the Lord, I noticed a reference to the prophets who were ashamed of what they had taught. They had been speaking and teaching as if their words were God's Words. Zechariah 13:4a-5a (NIV): *"On that day every prophet will be ashamed of his prophetic vision. He will say, "I am not a prophet."*

To be a teacher of God's word places a great responsibility on the teacher. I write with fear and trembling, praying for God's guidance in writing this study on the end times. I fear many teachers have been careless concerning what they imply is, "Thus saith the Lord". I believe that when the truth of the end times is fully revealed, many teachers and prophets will react similarly to these prophets spoken about in Zechariah chapter 13.

In closing, I believe what the Word of God plainly says and I will not put my trust in any teaching or a teacher of the Word of God who cannot back up his teaching with the plain speak Word of God.

11. Can we know when the Lord is actually coming ?

I do not believe we can know when Christ will return at this time, but I believe once a series of events start to happen, then, we can start to figure things out. In Matthew 24:36 (NIV): it says, *"No one knows about that day or hour..."* This is the verse that is often quoted as saying that no man knows when the Lord will return? The Bible says *"No man knows about that day or hour..."* of his return. It does not say that we would not know the year. Look at 1 Thessalonians 5:1-6 (NIV): *"Now brothers about times and dates, we do not need to write you, for you know very well that the day of the Lord will come like a thief in the night. While people are saying, "Peace and safety," destruction will come on them suddenly, as labor pains on a pregnant woman, and they will not escape."* **(Don't stop reading here like many who quote this verse, but read on.)** *"But you brothers are not in darkness so that this day should surprise you like a thief. You are all sons of the light and sons of the day. We do not belong to the night or to the darkness, so then let us not be like others who are asleep, but let us be alert and self-controlled."* If I am reading this correctly, the lost and those who are spiritually asleep will not recognize it is getting close to the time for the coming of the Lord. Christians who are awake and watching will see it coming, not the day or the hour, but, I believe, we will know the year, once it is about to happen!

Let me show you why I believe this. We have all heard the story of Noah. He was told to build an ark and get ready for God's judgment. He worked on the ark for about one hundred years. I imagine he took a lot of ridicule. Imagine hearing something like, "You are as slow as the Second Coming", except they were waiting for the flood. Well,

141

Noah did not know exactly when the flood was coming; he just knew he had to get ready. When he finished the ark, he still did not know the day or the hour of God's judgment, but he was ready. Then something happened that tipped Noah off that the Day of Judgment was at hand. When the animals all started showing up and started filling the ark, this began a chain of events that let Noah know that this was the year of the judgment of God. Once the ark was fully loaded with the animals, it was time for the rain.

Well, the Bible says in Matthew 24:36-39 (NIV): *"No one knows about that day or hour, not even the angels in heaven, nor the Son, but only the Father. As it was in the days of Noah, so will it be at the coming of the Son of Man. For in the days before the flood, people were eating and drinking, marrying and giving in marriage, up to the day Noah entered the ark."* This verse is not talking about Noah and his family. This verse is talking about those living in Noah's time that had rejected the Word of God through Noah's preaching. The unrepentant knew nothing about what would happen until the flood came and took them all away. That is how it will be at the coming of the Son of Man. If you go back and read Matthew 24:39-42, it is saying both the sinner and God's people will be going about their day. Then the Word of God warns the Christian in verse 42 to keep watch, so when the Lord returns they will not be caught off-guard. Just as the owner of a home, if he knew a burglar was coming, he would be waiting for him and not be caught off-guard.

Take a close look at this, it says no one knows the day or the hour, but it does not say one will not know the year. As I mentioned before, Noah knew something was up; he was not getting caught unprepared. He knew it was the year of God's judgment; because, God sent the animals to get loaded into the ark. Yet, when you read one book written by an international preacher, who has written many books on the

142

End-Times, he quotes this Scripture as saying, "...no man knows the day or the hour or the year..." This is not what the Bible says. It is sad that many Christians have been confused by teachers who are promoting a belief, by distorting the real meaning of God's Word.

If you study the opening of the seals in Revelation, chapter 6, you will see that the first seal is concerning the coming of the antichrist. When we see the events described in Chapter 6, it is as if we are starting a time-clock, to the seven years of the Great Tribulation. The Bible teaches that once the antichrist comes to power, he will, soon after this, make a seven-year peace with the nation of Israel. The beginning of this seven years of peace is probably a more accurate time for the start of the Great Tribulation.

The Great Tribulation is described in the book of Daniel in the Old Testament as Daniel's seventieth week. Historically, Daniel's seventy weeks were seventy weeks of years that were described in great detail, and history shows all were fulfilled except the last week of years, or the seven year period that is referred to as the Great Tribulation. This seven-year period is laid-out in the Bible with great detail. Some events are being described as happening within days from the start of these last seven years leading up to the coming of the Lord.

The following point needs to be explained to some who may be confused about the coming of the Lord. The actual coming of the Lord will happen when Jesus Christ returns upon the earth. He literally comes down to the Mount of Olives at the end of the Great Tribulation. There are references to the day of the Lord as being the day of the rapture. This is illustrated in 1 Thessalonians 5:2-3.(NIV): *"The day of the Lord will come like a thief in the night."*

143

The Bible bears out the event of Christ's coming in the rapture will not catch us who are waiting and watching by surprise as a thief **but only those who are not watching and ready. They will be caught unprepared, and Christ's coming will be like a thief in the night for them.**

STUDY POINT: Read Revelation 3:2-3 (KJV): *"Be watchful and strengthen the things which remain, that are ready to die. For I have not found thy works perfect before God. Remember therefore how thou received and heard, and hold fast and repent. If therefore thou shalt not watch, I will come on thee as a thief, and thou shalt not know what hour I will come upon you."* **This verse is referring to those <u>not</u> ready for Christ's return.** To them, Christ's return is coming as a thief in the night.

STUDY POINT: Read 1 Thessalonians 5:1-6 (NIV): *"Now brothers, about times and dates, we do not need to write to you. For you know very well that the day of the Lord will come like a thief in the night. While people are saying, "Peace and safety", destruction will come on them suddenly, as labor pains on a pregnant woman, and they will not escape.* ***But you, brothers, are not in darkness so that day should surprise you like a thief.*** *You are all sons of the light and sons of the day. We do not belong to the night or the darkness. So then, let us not be like others, who are asleep, but let us be alert and self-controlled."*

The key point to these Scripture verses is verse 4 above, **"But you brothers, are not in darkness so that this day should surprise you like a thief."** Then in verse 6, it really nails it: "Let us not be like others, who are asleep, but let us be alert." The Bible clearly tells us to be alert, watching and waiting for those last day events to unfold. Matthew 24:33 (NIV): says, *"Even so, when you see all these things, you know that it is near, right at the door."* Think about this verse. If we have to wait for these things to happen, it

144

is not imminent, but once they have happened, then it will be imminent. So you ask, what are these things for which we are to wait? Earlier, I showed the antichrist has to appear first; therefore, this verse above is talking about other things that must happen. What are those things?

Go back up a few verses to Matthew 24:29-31 (NIV): *"Immediately after the distress of those days, the sun will be darkened, the moon will not give its light; the stars will fall from the sky, and the heavenly bodies will be shaken."* One point I would like to add is the verse above gives a list of things that will happen after the distress of those days. What is the distress of those days that happens before these other things happen? If you remember in my chapter 7 on the coming antichrist, I show before the antichrist comes to power, the ten-region "One World Government" must be in place. And before all the governments of the world will give up their independence including the United States, we will experience some sort of event that will cause a global economic meltdown. This event will set the stage for the nations of the world to do whatever it requires to bring back order to our world. When the economies of the world collapse, this will certainly be some of the distress of those days for sure.

The Bible also talks about coming birth pains before the return of the Lord, the increase of many natural disasters around the world, including some of the severest earthquakes of modern times along with other natural disasters will certainly add to the distress of those days.

As I was reviewing my chapter called, "A possible scenario story leading up to the rapture", a truth about the coming antichrist and his desecrating the temple jumped out at me. It showed me that before the rapture can take place, the temple has to be rebuilt. I could not believe what I saw in God's Word, but it is there.

In closing this point, I believe we need to be watching and waiting for these events and prepare for what will happen leading up to this time. I believe these events will shake up our world, and before the rapture we will see the greatest revival the world has ever seen! These will be trying days and we need to be ready to share the gospel with the lost who will be coming back to God and turning to Christians, looking for answers to what is happening in our world.

Concerning our knowing the year of the Lord's return, I would like to share a thought I have had for some time. I wonder if maybe we can look forward to a year or a window of a few years that would make sense for the time-clock of the Tribulation to start ticking. I mentioned at the beginning of this section of my writings that I do not believe we can know the year of Christ's return at this time, but if you study the sixth chapter of Revelation regarding the opening of the seals, you will realize these seals mark the beginning of the Great Tribulation. Once the antichrist brokers a seven year peace with Israel and the Middle East, a seven-year timetable starts, and from thereon in, until the return of Christ to rule and reign on the earth, every event will happen in an orderly, timed, and predictable manner.

For more than one hundred years, people have tried to predict the return of the Lord and have been wrong. I recently heard a pastor say everything has happened, and the rapture should be upon us any time now. This statement has been worn out, and when the church hears this, they do not even blink. Think about this. If the rapture was going to happen on a certain month in two years and you knew that month, it would change your life; because, all of a sudden your retirement is not as important anymore. In fact, a lot of the things we look at as important would all of a sudden not be as important. Things of importance would be telling your friends and family about the coming of the Lord! However, because Christ's return is a big generational question mark, we do not even give this event much thought.

Back in the late eighties, a Christian sect wrote tracts and billboards and spread them everywhere entitled, "88 Reasons Why Christ Will Return in '88". They were so convinced, they sold all that they had and prepared for the coming of the Lord; some sold their homes and used the money to get the word out. Some had their pets put to sleep so that they would not starve when the rapture occurred. When the Lord did not return as they expected, they were quite embarrassed and scattered to many different churches, starting their Christian lives over again. The reason I am sharing this is, I want to talk about one of the points this group and others have used in error to predict the year of the Lord's coming.

In Matthew 24:32, it talks about the unfolding of end-time events and the fig tree. Many believe this is referring to the rebirth of the nation of Israel. This verse goes on to say, when you see these things; you know the Lord's coming is near, right at the door. Matthew 24:34 (NIV): further states, *"I tell you the truth, this generation will certainly not pass away until all these things have happened."* This sect of Christians and many other prophetic teachers over the years have believed the length of a generation that would not pass away until all these things happened was the forty year generation spoken of in the Old Testament. That generation died in the desert after forty years. When you consider that Israel was reborn as a nation in 1948 and add the forty year wilderness generation, this would add up to 1988. There is a real problem with using the forty-year generation in the wilderness; because, this was a generation under the judgment of God. If you read this story in the Old Testament, it says those who were under twenty years old were not held

147

accountable for the sins and decisions of their parents. They were not under judgment. But if you were twenty-one years old, in forty years you would die. Think about this, all those who were twenty-one years old in the wilderness would only live to be sixty-one years old. They would die young; because, their generation was under judgment.

The Bible says it has been accounted to man to live seventy years or more if he is strong. You see, the Bible tells us a generation is not forty, but seventy years. If you take the forty years in the wilderness and add in the twenty years for the young who did not have to die, then add in the ten years for those who were sixty and died young, then you are now back to the seventy year-generation or lifespan that God said we would live. If you now take the seventy years and add this to 1948, you have 2018. If this Christian sect that believed Christ was coming in 1988 had redone their calculations, then it would be 2018 based on a 70-year generation, and they were thirty years off.

Now I realize even if these calculations have merit, God does not have to hold to seventy years. The generation could be based on the fact that some live beyond seventy years. This would put things off to a future date. I really hope we have more time to get ready for the beginning of the Great Tribulation. Yet, if during the seven years of the Great Tribulation, God is doing everything in a predictable and timely manner, then it would make sense to me that God could use the seventy-year generation for the time frame leading to the return of Christ. In the next chapter I will show many coming events that fit into this soon coming window of time, illustrating how close we really could be to our Lord's return.

12. The window of the Lord's return

In this chapter, the thought I would like to explore concerns the prediction of the Lord's return or the start of the Great Tribulation coming during an eight year window of time from 2012-2020. Then as we approach the Lord's return, it may be possible to narrow the time down as we see the Great Tribulation actually getting started.

The Bible has predicted the rebirth of Israel along with other events, and one Bible prophecy says that when we see Israel reborn that generation would not pass away until the return of Christ. I did a study on the rebirth of Israel, showing why 1948 was the fulfillment of the rebirth of Israel, an event predicted in both the Old and New Testaments. In 1948 a window of the Lord's return was opened that was seventy to eighty years wide, the time of a generation. Sixty-four years of that window have been used. The Bible says, "No man knows about that day or the hour of the Lord's return."   However, the Bible also says in Luke 21:25-28 (NIV): *"There will be signs in the sun, moon and stars, on the earth, nations will be in anguish and perplexity at the roaring and tossing of the sea, men will faint from terror, apprehensive of what is coming on the world, for heavenly bodies will be shaken. At that time they will see the Son of Man coming on a cloud with power and great glory. When these things begin to take place, stand up and lift up your heads, because your redemption is drawing near."*

What is interesting is the number of events of a prophetic nature I have listed in the following pages that are falling into this window of time, 2012 - 2020. Below, I will cover this list of coming events that either are happening or could happen during this window of time.

1. You have the "2012" event that has been in the news about the Mayan calendar. The news media has said the Mayan calendar is predicting the end of the world. After some study on the internet, it turns out the calendar is just coming to its end and will reset to start again. Some are trying to say it is tied to solar events that coincide with the ending date of this calendar, but most who have studied this say the Mayans could not have known about these events.

We know as Christians, the world is not coming to an end in "2012", for the Bible says there will be one thousand years of peace on the earth after the return of the Lord. If you have watched the movie that was released recently, called, "2012", it could really put the fear of God in people. (Is it not strange that people will believe something like this, but they will not believe the Bible?) I believe as we get closer to this date, many people will be living in great fear. I believe people will take similar steps to what happened as the calendar approached the year 2000, causing the Y2K scare.

If these same people would read the Bible, they would realize it is the coming of the Lord for which they need to be ready. If you read about the last plague that God will pour out on the earth, the last of the bowl judgments, you will see what God has in store as his wrath in judgment for man's wickedness is far worse than what is depicted in the movie "2012".

Read Revelation 16:17-21 (NIV): *"The seventh angel poured out his bowl into the air, and out of the temple came a loud voice from the throne, saying, 'It is done.' Then there were flashes of lightning, rumblings, peals of thunder and a severe earthquake. No earthquake like it has ever occurred since man has been on the earth, so tremendous was the quake. The great city split into three parts, and the cities of the nations collapsed. God remembered Babylon*

*the Great and gave her the cup filled with the wine of the
fury of his wrath. Every island fled away and the mountains
could not be found. From the sky huge hailstones of about a
hundred pounds each, fell upon men. And they cursed
God."*

If you look at what is described in these verses, you will
see it describes the worst earthquake of all time, literally
being felt around the world! One great city, that some believe is Babylon, will be split into three parts. The cities of
the nations will collapse. Imagine the skyscrapers of every
city falling at the same time. Look at what happened to the
city of Port de Prince in Haiti. Imagine this happening to
cities around the world at the same time. Everyone would
be on their own; the death toll would be in the millions.
These verses go on to say that every island fled away. If
you think about it, most of the islands are volcanic in origin
and occur where there are weaknesses in the earth's crust,
often where the tectonic plates of the earth come together.
This earthquake, which God will use as part of his wrath on
the earth, will be so severe that it will be as if every conti-
nental plate on the earth is moved out of place at the same
time. It goes on to say the islands and the mountains will
disappear. Islands are just underwater mountains anyway.
This seems impossible; but the truth is if a quake is severe
enough and the shaking lasts long enough, it causes the
earth to turn into almost a liquid state. Buildings can actually sink into the ground. What is described here does not
even mention what will happen with the tidal waves which
will be generated by these quakes happening around the
world. These tidal waves may have a part in causing the
islands of the earth to disappear, almost like being washed
off the map.

Then after this happens, the Bible says the hail will come.
The King James Version of the Bible says these hailstones
will weigh a talent apiece or about 125 pounds. These will

be like bombs falling from heaven. Buildings not destroyed in the quake will be destroyed if hit with these hailstones. Yet it says man will curse God. How can you curse a God you do not believe exists? Well, the truth is, man knows there is a God, they just do not want to obey him. When God is done, man will have been given every opportunity to repent and will be without excuse when he stands before God on the Judgment Day.

2. A friend sent me a link to a site on the internet that talks about the return of the Lord happening in 2017 based on the year of Jubilee. The year of Jubilee being calculated to have occurred in 1917, the year England made a decree that the Jews would regain their homeland. Fifty years later in 1967, after winning the Six Day War Israel regained the city of Jerusalem and other lands that were part of Israel during the time of the Old Testament. The next year of Jubilee will be 2017. By the calculations of some scholars, this is the one hundred and twentieth Year of Jubilee or six thousand years since the creation of man. This would then lead into the one thousand years of peace that will happen after the Lord's Return during the Millennium. Again, this prediction falls into the 2012-2020 window.

3. Solar Flares: There are scientists predicting the next solar maximum will occur in 2012 and 2013. I went online and did some research on this coming event. I am not a scientist and do not want to be guilty of fear-mongering, but I have read several good articles on this coming event. I believe I have a balanced report. I would still encourage anyone to Google these events, and you can draw your own conclusions. The following thoughts are a brief outline of what they are saying.

One article I read said scientists have recently had growing concerns since the National Research Council gave a report funded by NASA and issued by the National Academy of

Sciences entitled, "Severe Space Weather Events". Scientists were concerned there could be a repeat of the eight day event that hit America in 1859 called the "Carrington Effect". This was a large solar flare accompanied by a coronal mass ejection, or CME, that threw billions of tons of solar plasma onto the earth's magnetic field, which disrupted the early electronics of its day. It basically burned out our telegraph system, even setting some telegraph offices on fire. In more recent years on March 13, 1989, six million people lost power in Quebec, Canada after a huge solar flare caused a surge from ground induced currents that turned the lights out for a day. Again, in 2003, it was said we missed the big one, but the solar storm caused satellites to fail, blackouts to occur, and some planes to be re-routed.

These solar storms occur about every eleven years. The next cycle should peak in late 2012 and early 2013. Scientists say a perfectly aligned solar flare could so affect our modern electronics it could take out our way of life for months. A top official from the European Space Agencies, space weather-head Mike Hapgood said, "I don't think the National Academy of Sciences report is scare mongering." He went on to say, "Scientists are conservative by nature, and this group is really thoughtful." He also said, "The NAS report is a fair and balanced report".

On the flip-side of the coin, you have another voice saying the earth is actually very well protected even if some satellites may not be. One report said when the earth is hit with a solar flare, the alignment of our magnetic field in relation to the sun and given the right conditions, solar flares could slide past the earth. Even if we do get hit with the big one, solar flares do not create an extinction event.

4. I was recently watching Perry Stone preach a message called, "Cosmic Prophecies in the Sun, Moon, and Stars". He was saying cosmic activity coming on the earth would

be announcing the Lord's return. Giving the following verses to back up this thought, Revelation 6:12-13, Matthew 24:29, and Joel 3:15, Perry Stone went on to say a certain kind of lunar eclipse will give a blood-red moon effect. He continued saying these lunar events have coincided with Jewish festivals and that these events have coincided with many events that have happened to the nation of Israel in its past history. In closing, he went on to say the eighth time one of these blood-red moon solar events will happen, will be in 2014-2015. Without actually saying it, he was giving the impression that the predicted events of the Book of Revelation could be tied to the events on these dates. Again, another prediction of end-time events is happening in the window of 2012-2020.

5. Are we headed for a world economic collapse? While economic leaders are trying to convince the public we have hit bottom and things will be improving shortly, many are not buying this. When the Great Depression hit America and the world in 1929, no one knew it would get as bad as it did until it did. When it looked like things would improve, the next shoe would drop. It basically took four years for the Great Depression to hit bottom in 1933, and it remained there until the Second World War. If we are following the same track, we may not hit bottom until 2012 or 2013. It could even take longer for this depression to hit bottom; because, we currently have programs in place that take away the sting of a depression to the unemployed. These were not in place in the 30's: welfare programs, food stamps, and unemployment compensation, to name a few.

We are currently printing and spending money like there is no tomorrow. Many states have run out of the money that is used to pay for the unemployed. The longer we postpone hitting the bottom in this economic downturn, the harder we will hit, and the longer it will take to recover. I believe a world economic collapse is irreversible, and I believe the timing of this horrible event will fall in this window of time, 2012-2020. I believe this event will lead to a One World Government.

I was reading a book by David Wilkerson called The Vision, written in 1974. So much of what was shared in this book has come to pass, and in light of current events, there was a page in his book that really caught my attention. From page 99, "...the United States of the World is just a world depression away. A collapse of the world monetary system could lead to a world government headed by a global dictator." The premier of Belgium recently said, "The method of international committees has failed." "What we need is a person of the highest order of experience, of great authority, of wide influence, of great energy, either a civilian or a military man, no matter what his nationality, who will cut all the red tape, shove all the committees out of the way, wake up all the people, and galvanize all governments into action. Let it come quickly...World anarchy and confusion can ripen this world for an antichrist dictator who will come in the name of peace to end the desperation and lawlessness that will abound."

More than ever, I see the stage is set for a world economic collapse. I believe the economies of the world are so fragile today that it will just take an event that will trigger a panic that will ripple an economic collapse around the world. Again, I believe this event could very well happen in the 2012 – 2020 window of time.

6. Another coming event that can play an important role in the prophetic calendar will be the next presidential election in 2012. It is generally accepted the current administration is trying its hardest to bring the United States into socialism, and this is only one step away from taking the steps to join the One-World Government. The current presidential administration's success in this agenda is very important.

The polls are saying this president's agenda is not getting the support it needs to complete his agenda, so the question arises whether the president can win re-election in 2012. If he were to lose this next election, the agenda to bring America into the fold of socialism and joining a One-World Government could be set back for many years.

I have a gut feeling we are approaching the time of the Lord's return, and if everything is coming together, then the question I have is whether this current administration can be taken out of office in 2012. I read a news bit on the web a couple of years ago about a few executive orders that were signed into law by a previous administration that gives the sitting president certain rights during a time of national emergency. Some of what I read said if America were thrown into a national emergency situation, the president, without congressional approval, could declare martial law, suspend the rights guaranteed under the Constitution, and delay a national election until things return to normal. I believe if we really are approaching the time-table for the setting up of the One-World Government and the system of the antichrist, there will be no stopping these events from happening. I believe some sort of terrorist or an event of nature could happen to allow the current administration to stay in power under these unknown rules. On the other hand, the state of the Union could be in such a bind that it would not matter who wins the next election. Again this coming election is falling into the window of 2012-2020.

7. I have given much thought as to whether or not I should include this next event in my book. I initially had a hard time getting good info on this topic until I recently watched a study on TV. It was entitled, "The Prophecies of the Popes", taught by a highly respected Bible teacher. I have since decided to include this topic in my book, and time will tell if I made a wise choice.

In the twelfth century, a Catholic Bishop named Saint Malachy living in Ireland, was summoned to Rome. While staying in Rome, it was reported that he had a vision of the future popes. The teacher who gave this study emphasized that these prophecies are certainly not equal to the prophecies of the Bible. Bishop Malachy made predictions concerning all the Popes in the future, leading up to the time of Christ's return. This document was lost for Three centuries in the Vatican archives, but since its discovery in the fifteenth century those predictions have been seen to be quite accurate. Saint Malachy predicted that there would be two hundred and sixty eight popes. The current pope, Pope Benedict is the two hundred and sixty seventh. He is in his eighties, and he could easily pass away during the 2012-2020 window of time. What is most interesting is the predictions concerning the two hundred and sixty eighth pope, the last pope before the return of Christ. It was predicted that he would be known as "Peter the Roman", and this last pope would work with the antichrist. I do not really know what part the pope is to play concerning the antichrist. I know there is one called the false prophet that will work with the antichrist. Could this be the pope? Time will tell.

8. One event I have touched on earlier in this paper that I believe is worthy of being included in the list of events that can fall into the window of 2012 – 2020 is the next big hit on America by Moslem terrorists. I already mentioned the Hiroshima project in which terrorists are planning to set off nuclear bombs in several cities in America at the same time. I hope this never happens, but it is a real threat. Our leaders have warned us it is not a question of if but a matter of when the next big hit will strike America. In 1993, terrorists attempted to bomb the World Trade Center. They did not succeed, but did they give up? NO! Eight years later they succeeded. It has been nine years since they succeeded with 911 and they are past due to strike us again. Terrorist groups are constantly feeding us false chatter to keep us spending money on security. The next big hit could easily happen in the next few years, and if this next terrorist hit comes while our economy is fragile, it could have a devastating effect on our country and the economies of the world.

9. I will include an event that does not have a time prediction with it, but it is believed it could fall into the 2012 - 2020 window. What is even more interesting about this event is it could be getting ready to be used by God as part of his plan for the Great Tribulation. This event is the Yellowstone Park "Super Volcano". This event was highlighted recently in the movie, "2012", anyone can go online and read more about this possible coming event. After studying this, there seems to be a consensus that Yellowstone is not ready to go any time soon, yet in January of 2010 the activity level has been increasing dramatically. The Yellowstone volcano's rim is about forty miles across with a magma pool the size of Lake Michigan under it. Scientists have been measuring rises in ground surfaces, and bulges are forming in more than one location. The biggest bulge is forming under Yellowstone Lake and has been measured to have grown one hundred feet in the last few years. This volcano has been estimated to have erupted every six hundred thousand years, and it is 20,000 years past due. Projections suggest an eruption would be catastrophic to the United States. It would cover most of the country with up to three feet of ash. By comparison the Mount Saint Helen's crater is about two square miles, but the Yellowstone volcano would create a crater of several hundred square miles!

The last eruption of the Yellowstone volcano is estimated to have spewed over eight thousand times the amount of ash as what Mount Saint Helen did in 1980. It would ruin the crops across the farm belt of America. A BBC feature on such volcanoes, said that after an eruption, "The sky will

158

darken, black rain will fall, and the earth would be plunged into the equivalent of a nuclear winter." The Cascade Volcano Observatory calls the Yellowstone Caldera, "...one of the largest and most active volcanoes in the world today."

The eruption of a volcano in Iceland caused high disruptions in air travel that has caused billions of dollars in damages, threatening to put airline companies out of business. The size of the Iceland volcano is so small compared to Yellowstone that it would be like comparing a marble to a basketball. If you read the following Bible verse, you will see why I believe this event may be what is being described in the Bible. Read Revelation 6:12 (NIV): *"I watched as he opened the sixth seal. There was a great earthquake. The sun turned black like sackcloth made of goat's hair, the whole moon turned blood red"*.

One last thought on the Yellowstone volcano from a quote in Time magazine by the geologist Paul Doss, who said, "An eruption could very well happen now, for the simple fact that nobody was around the last time it blew. So nobody knows what the warning signs are. There may be sporadic earthquakes, strange geyser patterns or a lifting of the surface, but nobody really knows."

In addition to these coming events that could be pointing to the return of Christ, there are many other events lining-up with the prophecies in the Bible that are signs God has given us to let us know it is time to "look up, for our redemption is drawing near".

In Conclusion, in the last few years, we have seen the coming together of the Revived Roman Empire along with a lot of activity toward establishing a One-World Government. As a sidebar to the coming One-World Government, a lot has been happening to bring the United States into this alliance of nations. Laws are being signed that are referred to as international laws, and we as a free country are now being told we are bound by these laws. These new international laws will take away the rights we are guaranteed Under the Constitution of this country. For some reason, our judges and government leaders are not doing a good job of defending our Constitution which they all swore to defend when they took the oath to serve our nation.

There have been laws and executive orders I have mentioned in this book of which I have given very little backup support. I do not want to be accused of promoting fear and conspiracy theories, but I feel I should name two of these laws that are now on the books and share a couple features of each. Google and research for yourself, to see if what I say is true. Laws are being put in place to allow our government to control the masses. The question is, "Why?" I believe the Bible teaches a global One World Government is inevitable. This leads me to believe that these laws are being put in place to reduce resistance from the people, when our government decides to join the coming One World Government. If you research the Patriot Act, you will see that our President can declare a national emergency at his discretion, and during this time of national emergency it would be a felony to possess more than one week's supply of food. If you control the food supply, you control the people. Also the John Warner Defense Authorization Act, (already signed into law) allows the President to declare a national emergency at his sole discretion which would tie the hands of Congress for six months before Congress can challenge this declaration. This law allows the President to take control of the National Guard in each state without the authorization of the governor of each state, and deploy them as he wills. Do not take my word for it. Look it up.

It has been said a One-World Government cannot work without the United States being a part of it. One of the
160

leaders behind the coming One-World Government has said if the United States dollar and economy collapses, they are prepared to bail us out under the condition that we will suspend our Constitution and come under the unified laws of the new One-World Government.

You know, if I were one who believed in conspiracy theories, it would be easy to believe that steps are being taken to cause the American dollar and our economy to collapse. The truth is our dollar and our economy are sliding in the wrong direction. We are praying for a turn-around, but many believe the fundamentals of our economy are in such trouble it is only a matter of time before we will see an economic collapse. The question is how long will it take? Some believe it could take a long time. The truth is our economy is so fragile all it would take is another 911 event or a large natural catastrophe to cause enough panic and economic disruption for a speedy collapse of our economy and the way of life that we have known in America. I believe it will be this type of a scenario that will weaken the resolve of Americans to keep our independence, thus making us willing to give in to the pressure of the new world system that will extend a helping hand to us.

One question I have to ask is, "Are two to ten years enough time to get everything in place for the antichrist to show up and for the Great Tribulation to start?" My answer is an absolute "yes!" You see, for the last several years, things have been happening in Europe that had to happen to pave the way for the antichrist. I think the biggest event to have happened has been the coming together of the European Common Market and the making of a common currency, the Euro. This makes all trade in these countries possible in one common currency. Well, this common currency has been growing in importance over the last several years. In fact, since 2002 to the present time, the value of the Euro has grown from being worth only eighty-eight cents to being worth as much as one dollar and fifty-seven cents compared to the U.S. dollar. Recently, the Euro has been rising and falling. The key point to realize is the world now has a second trade currency waiting in the wings. Up to the present time, the U.S. dollar has been the currency of choice for world trade. In fact, most oil trade and a lot of international trade is done in U.S. dollars. Some countries do not even have their own currency but trade in U.S. dollars.

In the last few years, the United States has been spending money that we do not have. We have also been buying more goods from other countries than what we are selling to them. This creates a huge world trade imbalance of which many Americans do not understand the ramifications. The bottom-line is, this out-of-control spending, huge trade imbalances and lowering of the interest rates has been making the dollar less appealing as a world trading currency! What is happening right now is most of our trading partners are losing money, holding onto U.S. dollars. If any bad economic event were to happen, like a global recession or another 911 event, our trading partners would be pressured into switching to a new global reserve currency.

With the Euro falling at this time, some wonder if the European Union will even survive. I believe there are powers working behind the scenes that will do whatever it takes to ensure the survival of the E.U. and a new One-World currency system. Even if it is not the present Euro, I believe, in the end, those who are working behind the scenes will look at America as expendable.

This brings up another huge recent event. Up until now, the countries of the Common Market have been using a common currency, but they have been self-governed. I read an article on the internet in 2008 stating the reason many countries are not switching to the Euro as their trading currency is because the Euro is a currency without a country to back it. If the EU countries were to do what the original thirteen U.S. colonies did in 1776 when we drew up a constitution and became the United States of America, the world would have a new confidence in this new super power to back up their currency. The United States of Europe under the leadership of one leader would give huge boost to the up and coming strength of the Euro as a currency and to this new country as a super power.

In 2008, the countries coming together under the umbrella of the Common Market voted on establishing a single leader to rule over the combined European countries. This vote took place, but it needed a unanimous vote to pass. One nation, Ireland, did delay it for a while, but a year later everyone signed-on. At first, this new power-block nation was voting on a new leader every six months. Now, even this has changed to a permanent leadership position. Now they have one country and one leader, leading a new country of over 500 million people. The Euro currency is positioning itself to be the New World currency. This new country is already talking about creating a system that will make their currency system a digital currency system that would require all of its citizens to have a computer chip implanted in the body. The technology is already in place, and they are saying that all the citizens of this newly formed country will have this implant sometime between 2012 and 2017. This being another event falling into the window of 2012-2020!

What we are seeing here is no longer the subject of end-time books and predictions we have heard preached so much for the last fifty years. These events are now coming to pass before our very eyes! We are now headed for the completion of the Revived Roman Empire that the Bible has predicted to take place before the Lord would return to rule and reign on the earth. Chapter 7, on the coming antichrist, shows why I believe the new One-World Government will be in place before the Great Tribulation starts.

After reading about all these things and the signs of the Lord's return just around the corner, **one can see a perfect storm brewing that can rapidly propel the world into the time called the Great Tribulation. Another way to put this is, we are on a collision course to the return of the Lord and just like the Titanic was unable to steer clear of the icebergs, we will not be able to avoid the forming of a One-World Government, the coming of the antichrist, and the coming of the Lord. These are not events that can be stopped through prayer, but they are events for which we need to be prepared! Now is the time to wake up and do all we can to win our lost friends and family! Jesus is coming soon.**

13. A possible scenario story leading up to the rapture

The following chapter is a fictitious story outlining how future world events could come together in just a few short years. It illustrates just how close we could be to the Lord's coming.

It is important that you read this chapter after you have read all previous chapters, for so much of what I am writing comes from the studies done in the previous chapters. I will be basing this scenario on Scripture as much as possible, but some will be conjecture on my part based on my study of the Word of God. God has not told me more than what I have found written in his Word. I do not claim to be a prophet and do not want to be stoned for not getting it right. I do believe that God could have given me some help in connecting the dots, but only time will tell if that is the case.

I believe where the Bible says this generation will not pass away until the coming of the Son of Man, is referring to the rebirth of Israel in 1948. I believe this statement is saying, some people of this generation will be living at the time of this event. This could be eighty years from 1948, so that would place the Lord's return somewhere close to 2028, but for my conjecture, I am going to use seventy years as the time of this generation. I will be looking at a window of the Lord's return as being between, 2012 - 2020. I could be wrong on the window of time I am using. The Lord's return may happen in the period of time following the years I have chosen, but because of the many coming events I have listed in this book that are falling into this window of time (2012 – 2020), I feel I must use this window.

The start of this scenario will be from a few years or so before the beginning of the Great Tribulation leading up to the rapture, which happens somewhere close to the middle of the Great Tribulation.

I have always believed America has stood in the way of the fulfillment of the end-time prophecies because of our being strong allies to Israel. We have blocked and hindered those who have had designs to destroy Israel. I have always believed that something has to happen to change the status-quo concerning this relationship or our ability to come to the aid of Israel. My script will be showing how America will be slipping from its position as a world military power and being the world cop who has been policing those who have stepped out of line.

2010

I will begin by summarizing where we are in America today. It is 2010; America's economy is going on the rocks. The powers that be are trying to convince us that the worst is over and we are on our way to a recovery. In reality, our real unemployment rate is approaching twenty percent, and we may very well be heading for a period of time that could be far worse than the Great Depression of the 1930's.

When the stock market collapsed in 1929, it took four years before we hit bottom. If this economic upheaval that we are currently experiencing has a similar track, we will not hit bottom until the fall of 2012. With stimulus strategies, the bottom could be postponed a bit further. I see the next shoe dropping between the end of 2010 to early 2011. It is a fact our economy is very fragile right now, and it is only being held up by degrees of global and domestic confidence. If anything happens to disrupt this weak confidence, the house of cards that is holding up our dollar and our economy could fall in short order.

2011

The American economy is turning downward in spite of all the efforts to turn it around. The year 2011 is turning out to be a year with a record number of natural disasters, both here, in America, and around the world. Countries around the world that are getting hit with disasters keep turning to America to help them rebuild. The money is running out as our economy continues to slip downward and more deficit spending is stacking up like snow on a mountainside waiting to set off an avalanche of trouble. We see inflation climbing up in many sectors as the Chinese currency gains value. Prices at Wal-Mart start to skyrocket. Global food crops have been challenged with many failures; this is causing the highest food inflation seen in our lifetime. America continues to be challenged by nations that are building up their armies. China, Russia and North Korea continue to flex their military muscles. The United States continues to use up our stockpiles of armaments, and our military infrastructure continues to wear down.

2012

We are now in 2012. Many people are living in fear and apprehension wondering where this year will lead us. Some people are getting ready for the end of the world like a previous Y2K craze. Food inflation is turning into a lingering problem, yet people are buying and storing food like they just heard a storm was to soon hit their area. Some people are storing food and supplies based on the predictions of the Mayan calendar. How do you get ready for the end of the world? I am so glad I can put my confidence in the Word of God which teaches that our Lord Jesus is coming back to rule and reign on this earth for a thousand years. After that we can look forward in all confidence to having an eternity with Christ and our loved ones.

Most people believe there is enough unrest for the national election this year to bring about a positive change in the administration. It is now October, 2012, just weeks away from the elections, when the United States is hit with a horrible terrorist event. The hit on America was comprised of many nuclear suitcase and dirty bombs that are set off in many cities in America and abroad on the same day. A second facet is biological in nature. A highly infectious agent is spreading across the land. The terrorists have simultaneously hit several cities, and air travel has spread the contagious agent before quarantines could contain it. The loss of life will be great, causing panic as everyone empties the food from store shelves all over America. Schools and businesses are shut down, and food deliveries are coming to a standstill. America is also hit in its water and electrical infrastructure. All this is happening in a forty-eight hour time frame. The hits in America and to our allies abroad are causing global fear and panic. Even the cities not affected by the terrorists are being hit by food shortages, riots and anarchy. This series of events is causing the world to question the future stability of the dollar, and we are seeing the beginning of its collapse. As we approach the national election of 2012, it seems our world is falling apart.

A little known set of presidential executive orders are used to declare martial law in the cities across America. The laws guaranteed in our Constitution are being suspended under the guise of helping to bring order back to America. The general election is postponed under another executive order. With food disruptions spreading, riots and anarchy are spreading to cities across America and the President calls for our military to come home to help restore order.

The positive news from these events is the churches of America are seeing record attendance. Many churches are witnessing true revival, as both the saints and the unsaved are repenting and seeking God with all their hearts. The

168

eyes of believers have been opened, almost like scales falling from their eyes. The church realizes God is giving us a window to reach the lost unlike any evangelistic opportunity in American history. God is using the global upheaval to plow the fallow ground and soften the hearts of millions to make them ready to accept the love of God through Jesus Christ. Now is the time for the church to step up to the plate. It is no longer about us; it is about reaching the lost while this window is open. Once the antichrist is revealed, he will quickly move to stop Christians from sharing the love of God. John 9:4 (NIV) says, *"As long as it is day, we must do the work of him who sent me. Night is coming when no one can work."*

2013

We are now at the beginning of 2013. The year 2013 is turning into another year of record-breaking natural disasters. Earthquakes of the highest magnitude are being felt around the world. The world gets hit with solar storms that are causing widespread technical blackouts. These solar storms are doing damage to satellites which are causing disasters no one dreamed would happen. One big mess caused by the solar disruptions of satellites is the off-shore oil derricks around the world that harvest oil under the ocean. Many are kept in place by GPS technology. This works with computers that control the propulsion units attached to the floating oil derricks. Once the GPS satellites quit working, the derricks start to float off their positions over the oil wells, and the underwater oil pipelines start to snap off. This starts causing multiple oil spills around the world. The blackouts put some metropolitan areas into total darkness for weeks causing great fear. Many people are turning to God. Churches are witnessing record attendance as masses of people, filled with fear are searching for answers and hope. Governments around the world are

coming down on the churches. The church in America realizes the day of corporate worship in a church building may
be coming to an end.

When it does not seem things could get worse with the
world's economies are on the verge of collapse and the
United States economy in a shambles, China, Russia, and
the Moslem nations abandon the U.S. dollar as their currency of international trade. This causes hyperinflation in
America. It also creates a situation similar to what happened in Germany in the 1920's. The banks there collapsed, and the banks in America are collapsing in the
highest numbers in history.

When the collapse of the dollar unfolds, some people who
invested in silver and gold are able to turn their investments
into inflated dollars and pay off their mortgages and debts.
Those who hold onto their silver and gold, thinking it will
be their salvation will discover once the dollar collapses
and food panic begins, those who have gold and silver
hordes, realize those who have food do not want gold.
Food ends up becoming like gold. Did not the Bible say
this would happen? Read Ezekiel 7:19, (NIV). *"They will
throw their silver into the streets, and their gold will be an
unclean thing. Their silver and gold will not be able to save
them in the day of the Lord's wrath. They will not satisfy
their hunger or fill their stomachs with it, for it has made
them stumble into sin."*

It is during this time, in the first half of 2013, that the
European Union is rising as the world's leading superpower, many nations around the world are aligning with the
EU, whose leader is calling for change. Things are so bad
there is little opposition to the great list of changes being
forced on the people of the world.

America's economy and military might are reduced to a fraction of its days of glory. It is during this time, around the end of 2013, things happen so fast. We have virtually seen the social and economic collapse of America, and we have seen a New-World order rise to power in Europe. It is during these times the governments and people of the earth are ready to accept any solution to these global problems.

Europe has come together as a One-World Government. Even in America, famine and anarchy are so widespread the masses of people are willing to accept whatever will bring these hard times to an end. It is during this time that ungodly American leaders will sweep the U.S. Constitution under the rug and sign a pact to join the New World Order. With what is happening with the rise of a new One-World Government in Europe, the saints are starting to wonder who the antichrist is. Many Christians are asking, "Why hasn't the rapture happened yet?" A key passage to understanding why is 2 Thessalonians 2:1-3 (NIV): *"Concerning the coming of our Lord Jesus Christ and our being gathered to him, we ask you brothers, not to become easily unsettled or alarmed by some prophecy, report or letter supposed to have come from us, saying the day of the Lord has already come. Do not let anyone deceive you in any way, for that day will not come until the rebellion occurs, and the man of lawlessness is revealed, the man doomed to destruction."*

A system of buying and selling is being instituted that encourages everyone to be implanted with a computer chip that will be like having a debit card built into your body. This system is being marketed as the technology that will save the economies of the world. Having this chip implanted starts off as a voluntary program. Under this new system, no one can cheat the government in the payment of taxes. Hard cash will be a thing of the past. Eventually this system will become mandatory, and if you do not receive

171

a chip, you will not be allowed to buy or sell. This computer chip is implanted under your skin, either on your right hand or on your forehead. Along with this implanted chip that is invisible, you are required to have a tattoo to mark you as having submitted to this system of the New World Order. It is during this time the new economic system makes all other currencies of the world worthless. Gold also becomes worthless under this system. All forms of bartering have been outlawed.

2014

Many Christians are wondering if the leader of this New World Government is the antichrist. It is March, 2014. There is much debate in the church about when the rapture is to happen, why it has not happened, who the antichrist is, and who is not the antichrist.

News reports hit the internet, and within minutes, over a billion people are glued to the internet or their television sets. It has just been reported that one of the ten leaders of the New World Order has been fatally wounded in the chest. It is reported that he is not expected to live. He holds on to life by a thread for three days in intensive care; the best doctors in the world are fighting to save this world leader. Then it is announced, on the third day, that he has died. The news travels around the world in minutes. Then a special interruption to the news comes across all news media. This world leader is not dead after all. He starts to breathe again, and miraculously, he comes back from death. His recovery is almost instantaneous. He is being interviewed, and it is apparent to all that something huge is happening. This once wounded leader is now talking about new plans that will bring order to this wounded world. This leader is up from his hospital bed announcing that God has healed him and given him an assignment of bringing salvation to the world and to usher in peace on earth.

One of the first actions he takes to bring about world peace is to broker a seven year peace between Israel and the countries of the Middle East. This treaty not only calms a global threat to world war, but it allows Israel to rebuild its temple beside the Dome of the Rock.

This leader's charisma and the tone of his voice is giving confidence in the minds of many who support him and putting fear in the hearts of any who would oppose him. (Revelation 13:3-4, NIV): *"One of the heads of the beast seemed to have had a fatal wound, but the fatal wound had been healed. The whole world was astonished and followed the beast. Men worshiped the dragon because he had given authority to the beast, and they also worshiped the beast and asked, 'Who is like the beast? Who can make war against him?"*

It is now that the antichrist is revealed beyond a shadow of a doubt. Most Christians thought the leader of the New World Government was the antichrist, but as it turned out, the antichrist was one of the ten world leaders under this One-World Government. He was wounded and arose as if from the dead on the third day, almost like the resurrection of Christ. Renewed debate ensues. Many are saying that he could not be the antichrist, for he did not have a mortal head wound. Some Christians actually believe that he is some sort of savior sent by God in answer to their prayers.

The first of the seven seals of the Book of Revelation has been opened. (Revelation 6:2, NIV): *"I looked and there before me was a white horse! Its rider held a bow, and he was given a crown, and he rode out as a conqueror bent on conquest."*

This leader is now recognized by most Christians to be the antichrist. The body of Christ recognizes at this time that a system of government is being forced on the world that is the system of the antichrist. Millions of Christians in America are standing together against these coming changes. Christian leaders are raising their voices against these changes that are coming from the pit of hell. A great revival is spreading, while at the same time many weak Christians are falling away and following after the new system of the antichrist that is unfolding around the world.

As the European Union is being consolidated and growing in power, regional and global panic is widespread, and it is during this time period that those in the church, who have been holding to a pre-Tribulation rapture, realize the Great Tribulation has begun. It is during this time a change is happening in the hearts of believers around the world. Some Christians are bitter at the thought the rapture has not happened, but the vast majority realizes God has a purpose in our being on the earth at this time, that is greater than our desire to be in heaven.

A great revival is breaking out at a time when persecution is rising; this is a time when so many have had their lives turned upside-down. It is during this time when all that this world has to offer is being pulled out from under us. We realize we must put our trust totally in our God. Christian's dependence on God is escalating. All of a sudden it is like the saints have recognized it is not about my needs and me, but it is about my lost neighbors, my wayward kids, and my grandkids. The believers are learning there is power in prayer and fasting. At a time when food is scarce, people are turning to God and miracles are flowing like a river from the throne of God. Some have said that the Holy Spirit would be removed during the Great Tribulation, they were so wrong; the world is witnessing the greatest outpouring of the Holy Spirit since the Day of Pentecost.

During this time, the corporate church is under attack. The antichrist has started his war on the saints, and laws are being passed that are forcing many churches to close their doors. Many churches saw the writing on the wall and took steps to move the church underground. Church cell groups have been organized, and believers are now moving into the privacy of their homes. They meet secretly yet continue to see record growth in total numbers. Believers are helping each other, and more miracles are happening now than what happened in the great church buildings now abandoned.

The situation around the world is just the opportunity for which many aggressive nations had been waiting. It is during this time of world chaos that China makes its move to take over Taiwan. North Korea invades South Korea. Russia takes back Georgia, the Ukraine, and other former territories. Other smaller less powerful countries are taking advantage of this time of global confusion and are waging war on weaker neighbors. Anarchy and civil unrest is causing death and destruction in so many countries around the world.

At this time Christians realize the second seal has opened. (Revelation 6:4, NIV): *"Then another horse came out, a fiery red one. Its rider was given power to take peace from the earth and to make men slay each other. To him was given a large sword."* With famine and starvation being widespread, governments are instituting rationing and trying to turn chaos into order. The world is truly ready for the antichrist to offer the world his plan of salvation and peace.

In close succession Christians realize the third seal has opened. Revelation 6:5-6 (NIV): *"When the Lamb opened the third seal; I heard the third living creature say, Come! I looked, and there before me was a black horse! Its rider was holding a pair of scales in his hand. Then I heard what sounded like a voice among the four living creatures, saying, 'A quart of wheat for a day's wages, and three quarts of barley for a day's wages, and do not damage the oil and the wine."* The world's food supplies are running out.

The fourth seal follows close behind the third, as millions are dying around the world. Wars are still widespread, famine is rampant, plagues, and sickness abound. These calamities and wars around the world are affecting one quarter of the earth's population. Revelation 6:8 (NIV), *"I looked and there before me was a pale horse! Its rider was named Death, and Hades was following close behind him. They were given power over a fourth of the earth to kill by the sword, famine, and plague, and by the wild beasts of the earth."*

2015

It is now 2015. Christian leaders are preaching and speaking out against what is happening. At the same time, more laws are being put in place to silence the voice of reason and the Word of God. Christian leaders are being rounded up, and horrible treatment of believers is happening behind closed doors to those who are being unjustly incarcerated. These attacks on the church start against its leaders and pastors. Soon it spreads to all Christians who are not going along with the new systems setup by the antichrist. During this time all people living on the earth must be implanted with a computer chip. This system starts as a voluntary system, but now you have few choices. You can choose to have this implanted in your forehead or on your right hand, you are also tattooed with a special mark to let all know that you have submitted to the rule of the antichrist. You cannot buy or sell without having this implant and the mark of the beast. Revelation 13:16 (NIV) says, *"He also forced everyone, small and great, rich and poor, free and slave, to receive a mark on his right hand or on his forehead, so that no one could buy or sell unless he had the mark, which is the name of the beast or the number of his name."*

It is a sad day as the masses around the world are taking the mark of the beast. Those taking the mark are turning in those who are standing against the antichrist. Even brothers and close friends and relatives are turning in those who are refusing the mark. Matthew 10:21-22 (NIV): says, *"Brother will betray brother to death, and a father his child; children will rebel against their parents and have them put to death. All men will hate you because of me, but he who stands firm to the end will be saved."*

The saints now realize the fifth seal has opened. Revelation 6:10-11 (NIV*), "They called out in a loud voice, 'How long, Sovereign Lord, holy and true, until you judge the inhabitants of the earth and avenge our blood?' Then each of them was given a white robe, and they were told to wait a little longer, until the number of their fellow servants and brothers who were to be killed as they had been was completed."*

Christians are standing up against the mark of the beast. The antichrist is giving orders to arrest any who refuse to bow to him and take his mark. The numbers being sent to prison camps is so great the camps cannot hold them. Mass trials are being held, truly a kangaroo court, for all are found guilty of being an enemy of the New World Order. What is happening to those deemed guilty is too gruesome to mention, but God is very much on the scene. God's word says "I will never leave thee or forsake thee", and God is giving his saints the grace they need to bear whatever is dealt to them. Read Daniel 11:32-33 (KJV): *"And such as do wickedly against the covenant shall he corrupt by flatteries: but the people that know their God shall be strong and do exploits. And they that understand among the people shall instruct many: yet they shall fall by the sword, and by flame, and by captivity, and by spoil, many days."*

2016

It is now 2016. It could be called the year the earth shook loose. The next event to take place is unlike any natural disaster to ever hit planet earth. A series of earthquakes shake the whole earth, almost as if every major fault line on earth were shifted. In America, major earthquakes shake and cause destruction from Los Angeles to Boston. The worst America sees from this series of quakes happens in Yellowstone Park. Scientists had reported a large lava lake the size of Lake Michigan, lying under parts of three states and Yellowstone Park. These scientists recently warned an eruption was overdue.

In a recent issue of National Geographic, they referred to the Yellowstone volcano as a "Super Volcano" saying an eruption could bring death and destruction, covering hundreds of square miles. They were right! It is the ash fallout doing the most damage. It is covering thousands of square miles. The whole breadbasket of America is being covered with several feet of ash in some places and several inches in others. The ash fallout is projected to last for weeks. During this time, the light from the sun is darkened to the point the temperature of the earth has dropped by fifteen degrees. Scientists are saying we will experience what is called a nuclear winter as a result of this event. The crops of wheat, corn, and other grains will certainly be destroyed. This ash is destroying the engines of cars and trucks. Panic and fear is griping America and the world as people realize much of the food crops have been destroyed.

At this time, the saints realize the sixth seal has been opened. Revelation 6:12-14 (NIV), *"I watched as he opened the sixth seal. There was a great earthquake. The sun turned black like sackcloth made of goat hair, the whole moon turned blood red, and the stars in the sky receded like a scroll, and every mountain and island was removed from its place."*

During this time, a period of escalating persecution is unfolding. However, during these trying times, the saints are coming together. The saints are so turned onto God, it is unbelievable. It is like the Book of Acts is repeating itself. Every miracle that happened when the church was born is being repeated, but many times over. Angels are releasing saints who are imprisoned. Miracles of provision are common, as saints who have food provisions share their food. They cannot give it all away, for God multiplies their provisions. It reminds me of this recent story I watched on the Sid Roth show where God lead a lady to take several suitcases full of clothes to African orphanages to help these children. Every time she tried to give the clothes away, more would appear in the suitcases. Finally, after visiting several orphanages, she dumped the suitcases into several garbage bags and left them behind with the orphanage workers. She arrived home and found all her suitcases were full again with children's clothes. This example of God's provision is proof that in the midst of the worst of times, God will show his own he will never leave them or forsake them.

At this time, before the seventh seal is opened, a number of supernatural things start to unfold. The saints begin to realize the Lord's coming for his saints is imminent. Millions are being saved. This is a glorious time to be alive and watch God's hand of mercy gathering in all the lost souls of the earth who will repent and turn to him. While we realize

God's hand of judgment is about to strike the earth, God's word says, *it is God's will that none should perish but that all would come to the knowledge of the truth.*

God is pulling out all stops to win the lost. This is also the time when angels are appearing in the heavens, proclaiming the gospel to the lost of the earth. When Christ arrived as a baby, angels heralded his coming, and now that he is ready to come again, the angels are back proclaiming his coming and preaching the gospel to the lost. Revelation 14:6-7 (NIV): *"Then I saw another angel flying in midair, and he had the eternal gospel to proclaim to those who live on the earth-to every nation, tribe, language and people. He said in a loud voice, 'Fear God and give him glory, because the hour of his judgment has come. Worship him who made the heavens, the earth, and the sea and the springs of water."*

During this time, the hardest hearts of sinners are melting and crying out to God for mercy. Thieves, prostitutes and all kinds of sinners are turning to Christ. What is sad is there are so many church-goers who are turning bitter towards God, instead of drawing closer to him during these hard times.

During this time, all those on the earth must make their choice. Do they want the meal ticket the antichrist is offering or do they want to press into God and patiently wait for the Lord to take them home. Revelation 13:9-10 (NIV) says, *"He, who has an ear, let him hear. If anyone is to go into captivity, into captivity he will go, if anyone is to be killed with the sword, with the sword he will be killed. This calls for patient endurance and faithfulness on the part of the saints."*

The angels are proclaiming to the lost a last warning for the world to reject the mark of the beast or face eternal judgment. Revelation 14:9-11 (NIV), *"A third angel followed them and said in a loud voice: 'If anyone worships the beast and his image and receives his mark on the forehead or on the hand, he too, will drink of the wine of God's fury which has been poured full strength into the cup of his wrath. He will be tormented with burning sulfur in the presence of the holy angels and of the Lamb. And the smoke of their torment rises forever and ever. There is no rest day or night for those who worship the beast and his image, or for anyone who receives the mark of his name.'*

These are exciting times. So many lost souls are choosing Jesus over the antichrist. It is a sad time as well because many have not made the right choice and have just not taken God seriously. Only God knows the heart of man, and only he will be able to justly sort out those who are ready to go and those who will be left behind. The Word of God is about to be fulfilled. Revelation 3:15-16 (NIV): *"I know your deeds that you are neither cold nor hot, I wish you were either one of the other. So because you are lukewarm, neither hot nor cold, I am about to spit you out of my mouth."*

It is sad so many lukewarm saints do not recognize what is taking place. They have held onto all the world has to offer and will not let go to grasp all God has to offer. Revelation 3:17-19 (NIV): says, *"You say, 'I am rich: I have acquired wealth and do not need a thing.' But you do not realize that you are wretched, pitiful, poor, blind and naked. I counsel you to buy from me gold refined in the fire, so you can become rich; and white cloths to wear, so you can cover your shameful nakedness, and salve to put on your eyes, so you can see. Those whom I love, I rebuke and discipline, so be earnest and repent."*

Is it not interesting when God was getting ready to pour out his judgment on Sodom and Gomorrah, Abraham interceded for the righteous? But now, in these last days, it is Jesus who is interceding for the unrighteous, and he is using all means at his disposal to evacuate those who belong to him before the wrath of God falls. In the Old Testament, angels came and ushered the righteous out of harm's way, and now, just before the harvest of the earth, angels are showing up to give the lost sinners one last chance to accept Jesus Christ.

2017

It is now early in 2017. Wow! It is happening! The 144,000 specially chosen Jews are being visited by angels and are given a seal which sets them apart to do a special mission for God. They are also empowered to do this special assignment for God. It is their job to bring the message of Christ to all the Jews around the world. This job would be impossible in these times of world upheaval, except that they are being equipped for the job. The 144,000 are given their resurrected bodies, and they are showing up everywhere, supernaturally. The antichrist cannot stand in their way. The Jews are being led to Christ in great numbers, but sadly, many Jews are still not yet convinced.

After the rapture, the 144,000 Jews will be warning the Jews left behind due to their indecision to accept Christ, to flee to Israel to escape the wrath of God that is coming soon. Jerusalem has been living under a period of peace established by the antichrist. The temple has been under construction and almost completed. The news media has been instructed to ignore any news events of a supernatural nature. The antichrist is trying to keep control of the news. The internet has government filters that make it hard to get the whole truth of what is happening around the world

Israel has been living during a time of unprecedented peace, a peace that allowed them to rebuild their temple. It seems this period of peace, brokered by the antichrist may be coming to an end. During a time that Israel has had its guard down, their old enemies have been plotting to attack. Ezekiel 38:10-11(NIV): *"This is what the Sovereign Lord says: On that day thoughts will come into your mind and you will devise an evil scheme. You will say, "I will invade a land of unwalled villages; I will attack a peaceful and unsuspecting people—all of them living without walls and without gates and bars."*

Then it happens; the battle of Gog and Magog breaks out. The might of the Russian army is amassing on all sides, along with many nations who want to see the destruction of Israel. There is no doubt about what is about to happen. In many ways, it is similar to what happened fifty years before, when Israel fought the Six-day War. At that time, the enemies of Israel were very formidable, and it looked like there was little hope for Israel. The United States was taking a hands-off policy under President Johnson. They had supplied them with armaments but would not send troops or air support. Israel decided their only hope was to launch a preemptive strike against their many enemies. In six days, they had their enemies ready to sign a peace treaty. They had claimed the West Bank, the Golan Heights, and the Gaza Strip, along with the rest of Jerusalem that was still under Arab control. It truly was a year of Jubilee.

Now 50 years later, will this be the next year of Jubilee? Some Bible scholars do believe this year is to be the next year of Jubilee. This battle may determine if they are right. The war of Gog and Magog is about to break out. It is evident the United States will not give support of any kind. Israel recognizes it must reach out for help from another source. The 144,000 Jewish evangelists have told many in Israel that God will deliver them, and their deliverance will not come from the hand of man.

During this time the two witnesses spoken of in the Book of Revelation show up in Jerusalem. What a stir they are making. They are giving a message of hope to Israel, letting them know that the God they serve is bigger than any army in this world and that God's Son, Jesus Christ is their real Savior. The war breaks out, and the world is watching. Many believe this will be the end of Israel. The saints know the Lord is coming for them soon. Many of the ranks of the saints have been slain by the antichrist, but those who remain are on their knees calling out to God for Israel's deliverance. There are more than just the troops of Israel's army on the move. The armies of God, led by Michael, the archangel are pressing an attack that is unseen but very much felt by the Russian army. The Russians are confused, and a spirit of fear permeates their ranks. The panic is such that many thousands of Russian soldiers die in the night at the hands of their comrades. As morning arrives, the armies of Gog and Magog find real reason to fear, as weapons they never dreamed existed are raining destruction on them. In fact, it is such a miraculous defeat that when the battle is over, and as news spreads of the utter destruction of one of the largest armies in the world, tens of thousands of Jews, Muslims and Gentiles around the world are coming to Christ. The antichrist is angry, and he knows his time is short. Read Ezekiel 38:21-2 (NIV): *"I will summon a sword against Gog on all my mountains, declares the Lord. Every man's sword will be against his brother. I will execute judgment upon him with plague and bloodshed; I will pour down torrents of rain, hailstones, and burning sulfur on him and on his troops and on many nations with him. And so I will show my greatness and my holiness, and I will make myself known in the sight of many nations. Then they will know that I am the Lord."*

God has opened the eyes of his people Israel and they are coming to Jesus Christ in great numbers. WOW! Our God reigns!

184

The work of the 144,000 Jewish evangelists is having tremendous results. Thousands of Jews are accepting Christ as their Messiah. The rapture is about to happen. It is evident God is harvesting his special chosen people the Jews to be a part of the bride of Christ. It is hard to believe after such a display of God's majesty, power, and love for the nation of Israel that many Jews will still reject Christ as their Messiah and will be left behind. When Jesus Christ comes for his bride, those Jews who have still rejected him will mourn as they realize they have rejected Christ for the second time! The first time was when Jesus went to the Cross for them, and now, when he comes back for them in the rapture.

Read Matthew 24:30-31 (KJV): *"And then shall appear the sign of the Son of Man in heaven: and then shall all the tribes of the earth mourn, and they shall see the Son of Man coming in the clouds of heaven with power and great glory. And he shall send his angels with a great sound of a trumpet, and they shall gather together his elect from the four winds, from one end of heaven to the other."*

Now it is safe to say the Lord's return for his bride is imminent. It is now the week of the Feast of Trumpets. It is the end of September, 2017. The antichrist has waged a relentless war against the saints for three and one-half years. Now, read Daniel 7:25 (NIV): *"He will speak against the Most High, and oppress his saints and try to change the set times and the laws. The saints will be handed over to him for a time, times and half a time."*

To satan's frustration, the saints have stood the test, and they have kept the faith. The words of Paul found in 2Timothy 4:6-8 (NIV) are so fitting. *"For I am already being poured out like a drink offering, and the time has come for my departure. I have fought the good fight, I have*

185

finished the race, I have kept the faith. Now there is in store for me the crown of righteousness, which the Lord, the righteous judge, will reward me on that day, and not only me, but also to all who have longed for his appearing."

The Bible says no one knows the day or the hour of his coming, but the saints feel it is time to look up, for our redemption is drawing near. During the Feast of Trumpets, the children of Israel were to wait for a loud trumpet blast, which would mean it was time for them to be led to the Mountain of God. Read Exodus 19:16-17 (NIV): *"On the morning of the third day there was thunder and lightning, with a thick cloud over the mountain, and a very loud trumpet blast. Everyone in the camp trembled. Then Moses led the people out of the camp to meet with God."*

In the New Testament, it says we are to wait for the last trumpet. It will not matter what we are doing, whether we are asleep in the night or awake when the trumpet sounds. All the saints who are ready and waiting for the Lord's return will hear the trumpet, and in the twinkling of an eye, we will be out of here. Read, 1 Thessalonians 4:16-18 (NIV): *"For the Lord himself will come down from heaven, with a loud command, with the voice of the archangel and the trumpet call of God, and the dead in Christ will rise first. After that, we who are still alive and left will be caught up with them in the clouds to meet the Lord in the air. And so we will be with the Lord forever. Therefore encourage each other with these words."* So instead of Moses leading us to meet God at the last trumpet, this time Jesus will come to take his bride to meet his Father in Heaven.

The awaited Rapture has happened

There is no doubt Israel and all of God's chosen elect have come out on top after this battle, but the antichrist is about to launch his next attack against Israel. God has just removed his saints from the reach of the antichrist, the new temple has just been rebuilt and dedicated in Jerusalem. After the battle of Gog and Magog, the antichrist shows up and visits the temple with much fanfare to announce to the world he is the savior and god of this world.

I would encourage you to read all of Mark 13:14-27. I will write out the first and last verses of this sequence of verses Mark 13:14, 27 (NIV*): "When you see the abomination that causes desolation standing where it does not belong - let the reader understand - then let those who are in Judea flee to the mountains." "And he will send his angels and gather his elect from the four winds, from the ends of the earth to the ends of the heavens."*

If you will carefully read the above verses, Mark 13:14-27, you will see that the rapture occurs after we see the abomination that causes desolation standing where it does not belong. The Bible says when you see the antichrist standing in the temple this will be the time of the rapture. If the temple has not been rebuilt and the antichrist has not arrived at the temple, then the rapture cannot occur until these events happen, according the God's own Word. If you will read Daniel 9:27, you will see the timing of this event. Daniel 9:27 (NIV): *"He will confirm a covenant with many for one 'seven', but in the middle of that 'seven' he will put an end to sacrifice and offering. And one who causes desolation will place abomination on a wing of the temple until the end that is decreed is poured out on him."*

To me this is plain speak. If the seven is the seven years of the Great Tribulation and in the middle of the seven years is three and one half years, then when you take Mark 13:14,27 and Daniel 9:27 together, God's word plainly says that the rapture will happen in the middle of the Great Tribulation.

After the rapture, there is a great leadership vacuum in Israel, because many Jews accepted Christ as their savior and went up in the rapture. This has given the antichrist the opportunity he desired to make his move and set himself up as the god of this world. He just does not quite get it. Jesus is coming back and satan will lose.

2017 – 2020

The rapture has happened. The bride of Christ has now been led to the throne of God, and a great celebration is happening. All those who would decide to make Christ their Lord, have made that decision. Jesus waited until all who would accept him made the right choice. Those people left behind are the ones who will later curse God as the wrath of God comes upon the earth and mankind.

Many Jews and Muslims accepted Christ as their Messiah before the rapture, as they are also an important part of Christ's bride. Those Jews who did not make that choice will have a hard time as the antichrist breaks his seven-year peace pact with Israel. The antichrist makes a shrewd decision not to make war on the Jews while at the same time he has been going after the saints. His peace pact with Israel makes it possible for him to focus his attention on the saints, and it gives the Jews a period of peace to rebuild the temple.

After the rapture, the antichrist is left very frustrated, as the saints have been taken out of his reach. The 144,000 Jewish evangelists are working hard now to help warn and get the Jews around the world to a place of safety in Israel. Revelation 18:4 (NIV): says, *"Then I heard another voice from heaven say, "Come out of her my people, so that you will not share in her sins, so that you will not receive any of her plagues."* All hell is about to break loose as God pours out his wrath on the earth and unrepentant man. After a time of great celebration at the Marriage Supper of the Lamb, the Bride of Christ will come back with Jesus Christ for the grand finale at the battle of Armageddon. Jude 14 (NIV): *"Enoch the seventh from Adam, prophesied about these men: see the Lord is coming with thousands upon thousands of his holy ones."*

What totally amazes me is: after the battle of Gog and Magog, where God showed the world what would happen to any nation who would try to attack God's chosen people the Jews, the nations of the world are about to try it again. This time, Jesus himself, will lead the army that will put down all attempts to hurt Israel for the next 1000 years.

If you would read all of chapters 12-14 in Zechariah, you would see a complete picture of God's battle plan for the nations who would attack Israel, and you will see the ushering in of the millennial reign of Christ. What I will do is piece together some of the important verses from these three chapters, so you can see the unfolding of God's plan for both Israel and her enemies. What I am sharing here is not a scenario story; this is a commentary straight from God's Word.

I will start off with God's unshakable promise of protection for Israel. Zechariah 12:1-5 (NIV): *"This is the word of the Lord concerning Israel. The Lord, who stretches out the heavens, who lays the foundation of the earth, and who forms the spirit of man within him, declares: "I am going to make Jerusalem a cup that sends all the surrounding peoples reeling. Judah will be besieged as well as Jerusalem. On that day, when all the nations of the earth are gathered against her, I will make Jerusalem an immovable rock for all the nations. All who try to move it will injure themselves. On that day I will strike every horse with panic and its riders with madness," declares the Lord. "I will keep a watchful eye over the house of Judah, but I will blind all the horses of the nations. Then the leaders of Judah will say in their hearts, 'The people of Jerusalem are strong, because the Lord Almighty is their God. On that day men will be stricken by the Lord with great panic. Each man will seize the hand of another, and they will attack each other."*

These verses sound similar to what happens at the battle of Gog and Magog. But as you continue to read in your Bible, you will see the Lord is ushering in the 1000 years of peace. You will see that only a remnant totaling one third of those Jews who were left behind in the rapture will survive to live into the millennium. This one third, who do survive these times, will totally turn back to the Lord in tears realizing they were wrong.

Zechariah 12:10 (NIV*): "And I will pour out on the house of David and the inhabitants of Jerusalem a spirit of grace and supplication. They will look on me, the one they have pierced, and they will mourn for him as one mourns for an only child, and grieve bitterly for him as one grieves for a first born son."*

In closing, the last 2 verses I use will be shortened for brevity, but if you will read these chapters yourself you will see I am staying true to the intended meaning. These verses show that the Lord is coming back to establish his Kingdom on earth.

Zechariah 14:3-4b (NIV): *"Then the Lord will go out and fight against those nations, as he fights in the day of battle. On that day his feet will stand on the Mount of Olives."*

Zechariah 14:5b (NIV): *"Then the Lord my God will come, and all the holy ones with him."* **Praise the Lord, may you come quickly. We Win.**

190

14. What can we do to prepare for Christ's coming?

If this study makes sense to you, we are fast approaching the coming of the Lord and we will be going through part of the Great Tribulation. It begs the question; "What can we do to prepare for this time?" I will outline a few important steps we can take to prepare for what is coming soon.

1. Have you accepted Jesus Christ as your Savior? If your answer is, 'yes', then the question is, "Are you living the Christian life to your full potential?" During these last days, God wants to use us to our fullest potential, and we must press in to seek God with all our hearts. Do some soul searching. This is where we have to really be honest with ourselves; we cannot hide anything from God. Do you have habits and sins that would be displeasing to God and hinder God from using you?

As I bring this study to a close, I have felt the Holy Spirit leading me to include a study on the parable of the ten virgins. Jesus told this parable during his ministry on earth. It is found in Matthew 25:1-13, Jesus was teaching his disciples when they asked him questions recorded in Matthew 24:3 (NIV): *"As Jesus was sitting on the Mount of Olives, the disciples came to him privately. 'Tell us,' they said, 'when will this happen, and what will be the sign of your coming and the end of the age?"* Jesus went on to teach his disciples about his coming in chapter 24 (much of it is in what I call plain-speak). When Jesus taught his disciples as recorded in chapter 25, He spoke in parables. Jesus' disciples asked him questions written in Matthew 13:10-11 (NIV): *"Why do you speak to the people in parables?" This was his reply, "The knowledge of the secrets of the*

kingdom of heaven has been given to you, but not to them."
Jesus went on to say, *"There are those who have become calloused, and the truths of God's word are hidden from them."*

I have given this brief explanation on what a parable is because many parables are hard to understand and not all are explained in the Bible. I believe the parable of the ten virgins holds many insights concerning what will be happening at the time of Christ's return for his bride. I will write out the whole parable and give a brief running commentary on some of the message I believe God wants us to understand as we approach the time of Christ's return for his bride.

Matthew 25:1-13 (NIV): says, *"At that time the kingdom of heaven will be like ten virgins who took their lamps and went out to meet the bridegroom. Five of them were foolish and five were wise. The foolish ones took their lamps but did not take any oil with them. The wise, however, took oil in jars along with their lamps. The bridegroom was a long time in coming, and they all became drowsy and fell asleep. At midnight the cry rang out: 'Here's the bridegroom! Come out to meet him!' Then all the virgins woke up and trimmed their lamps. The foolish ones said to the wise, 'Give us some of your oil; our lamps are going out.' 'No,' they replied, 'there may not be enough for both us and you. Instead, go to those who sell oil and buy some for yourselves.' But while they were on their way to buy oil, the bridegroom arrived. The virgins who were ready went in with him to the wedding banquet. And the door was shut. Later the others also came. 'Sir! Sir!' they said. 'Open the door for us!' But he replied, 'I tell you the truth, I don't know you.' Therefore keep watch, because you do not know the day or the hour."*

To start off, I did a study on the significance of the number ten. According to Jewish custom, if you have ten Jews living together you have a congregation, and you can build a synagogue. This truth indicates to me that Jesus was talking about the church as well as a Jewish synagogue. With this in mind, you realize Jesus was saying at the time of the end, when the church is waiting for his coming, many in the church will have similar traits to the ten virgins. There is much significance to the fact they were carrying lamps that needed oil to be ready for the bridegroom's return. The lamps were the vessels that held the oil. When you study the Bible, you learn the oil is symbolic of the Holy Spirit, and we are the vessels in which the Holy Spirit lives.

This Parable says the five foolish virgins did not even have any oil. As Christians, the oil of the Holy Spirit is what gives us our power and strength to live the Christian life. I believe that those believers who do not have any oil are not taking their walk with God seriously. They may be going to church, but they are really just going through the motions.

When the Bible says the bridegroom was a long time in coming, I believe it is saying Christ's return has not happened as soon as many expected. I believe, after having done this whole study on the end-times that the eighty to ninety percent of American Christians who have been taught Christ is coming before the antichrist arrives and then the seven-year tribulation starts will be in for a big surprise. I believe the strongest message from this parable is for those who are not taking their walk with God seriously and will be too weak to make it to the end.

Job in the Old Testament story went through the greatest tribulation any man has ever had to suffer. His wife even told him to just curse God and die. Many a man in his day would not have stayed true to God, but Job's walk and faith in God was stronger than any storm or trial that came his way. I believe many Christians going through the coming tribulations of the last days will only make it because they will have an inner strength from the Spirit of God similar to what Job had. This strength of spirit can only be developed by spending time with God in his word and in prayer. Just showing up at church once a week will not develop the strength of spirit we will need to weather the storms ahead.

My last closing thought may raise some eyebrows, but I will speak my mind, for I believe what I am about to say, needs to be said. At the end of the parable when the five foolish virgins went on their way to find the oil they needed and later came back wanting to enter the marriage supper, Jesus said, *"I tell you the truth, I don't know you."* **As I was studying this, I wondered what could the five foolish virgins have done that was so bad that they would be so totally rejected. What this parable is saying is, many people in the church will not make it into the Kingdom of God. In fact it shows that 50 percent will not make it. <u>This is serious</u>. What can this possibly mean?**

As I have studied and prayed over this, I have come up with only one answer. The Bible talks about a sin that is unpardonable. It is referred to as blasphemy against the Holy Spirit. I have heard teaching that considers taking one's own life is also unpardonable. Well, I believe in the last days there is another unpardonable sin and that is to take the mark of the beast. I believe, in the last days, when we are going through the tribulation of those days, before the wrath of God begins, this portion of the last days will be a time of testing for Christians unlike anything we have ever seen here in America. I believe the weight of Scripture shows the church will have to make the choice of whether or not to accept the antichrist's system. We will be amply warned not to take the mark of the beast, but I believe many churches are so full of weak Christians, and many of these will say God would not expect them to go hungry and die. I believe they could be easily deceived into believing the antichrist is their savior and go along with his system. The   bottom line is, unless we are full of the Spirit of God and have the strength of the Spirit that will carry you through these times of trials and tribulations that lie ahead, we could end up being like the foolish virgins who do not make it into the Marriage Supper of the Lamb. I am listing a few Scripture references below that go along with what I am saying in this study on the ten virgins. I encourage you to look them up and see if what I am saying is possible.

God warns the Saints not to take
the mark of the beast..............................Revelation 14: 9-12

Why the Lord delays his coming..........................2 Peter 3:9

God warns Saints to be patient................Revelation 13:9-10

War on Saints to last three and one half years...Daniel 7:25

If you have not accepted Jesus as your Lord and Savior, these easy steps will put you in right standing with God.

1. Admit you are a sinner and repent.

   (Romans 3:10 NIV), *"As it is written: there is no one righteous, not even one."*

   (Romans 3:23 NIV), *"For all have sinned and fall short of the glory of God."*

   (Luke 5:32 NIV), *"I have not come to call the righteous, but sinners to repentance."*

2. Believe in the Lord Jesus Christ.

   (John 3:16 NIV), *"For God so loved the world that*

he gave his one and only Son, that whosoever believes in him shall not perish but have eternal life."

3. Confess or declare that Jesus is the Lord of your life.

(Romans 10:9 NIV), *"That if you confess with your mouth, 'Jesus is Lord,' and believe in your heart that God raised him from the dead, you shall be saved."*

The sinner's prayer

If you would like God to forgive all your sins and make Jesus Christ the Lord of your life, then stop here and say this prayer to God. (Prayer is simply talking to God.)

Dear Heavenly Father, I know I am a sinner. I believe Jesus Christ died on the cross for me. Please forgive me of all my sins. Jesus, please come into my heart and wash my sins away. Please be the Lord of my life and help me to live for you every day. I ask this in Jesus name. Amen.

The Bible says when a sinner repents and makes Jesus his Lord, the angels in heaven rejoice.

A word of warning is advised at this point. As we read in the story of the ten virgins, not all who call themselves Christians will make it to heaven. Knowing about Jesus and the plan of salvation is no guarantee of making it to heaven. When we arrive in heaven, the greatest surprise will be seeing people we did not think would make it. And just as surprising will be the absence of those we thought would be there. The Bible says Jesus knocks on the door of our hearts and wants to come in and live with us. The important thing to realize is God wants our hearts, not just our minds. Head knowledge about salvation does not save us, but sincerely allowing God to forgive and wash our sins away will allow God to give you a new heart. When your heart is changed, people will notice you have been changed and made into a new person in Christ. This is called being "Born Again."

I would like to share a story from a recent conversation I had with a young man who believes we really are close to the Lord's return. He told me he would never take the mark of the beast. Yet he believes its ok for him to live with his girlfriend and go out and get drunk from time to time. He has what I call designer faith. It is NOT based on the pure Word of God, but it's based on what seems good to him. What a shame it would be for someone to go through the Tribulation of the last days and refuse to take the mark of the beast and then still not make it into the Kingdom of Heaven because they did not have a true Born Again experience, based on the Word of God.

As a new believer your next step would be for you to find a network of believers to help you grow in the Lord. Finding a good church is a good place to start.

2. Is your financial house in order? This question requires taking steps to streamline your budget and get out of debt if at all possible. Even Christians have been wasting money and living beyond their means. Based on my study of God's word I believe the beginning of the Great Tribulation could be only three to seven years away. When I started this study two years ago, I realized I had assets I could use to help me get out of debt. I went through my credit card bills and looked for recurring monthly bills I could cut from my budget. I personally eliminated 300 dollars a month through this process. A lot more can be said in this category, but the bottom line is, as we approach the Lord's coming we will witness the world and society being turned upside down as we know it. The opportunities to witness to the backsliders and the lost will be tremendous. Those who get their financial house in order will be in the best position to reach out to the lost during these times.

Under the subject of finances, I cannot believe how many financial advisors are telling people to put their resources into gold and silver. I do not believe we will ever see gold and silver become the medium of exchange in America or the world. How do you split a gold coin to buy food? If you think about it; the thing really drives up the value of precious metals is fear the value of our currency will collapse and become worthless. This did not even happen during the great depression. Now I am not saying this could not happen. In fact, I believe we are heading towards a global economic collapse, and this event will lead to the formation of a one-world government. I believe this event must happen before the antichrist can rise to power. So, as a Christian, I want to know what God's Word has to say about my investments. Ezekiel 7:19 says that *"they shall cast their silver in the streets and their gold shall not be able to deliver them in the day of the wrath of Lord. They shall not satisfy their souls, neither fill their bowels."* Then read Zephaniah 1:18 (NIV): *"Neither their silver, nor their gold, will be able to save them on the day of the Lord's wrath."* Think about this, as we approach the Lord's coming and the global famines that will take place as described in the opening of the seals of Revelation 6, people who have prepared and have food will not want your gold for their food. As Ezekiel 7:19 says, *"..they shall not satisfy their souls, neither fill their bowels..."* Bowels are your belly. To me, God's Word is saying it is wiser to have food for your belly then to have gold. You could even say during these coming hard times food will be gold.

The other day I was reading headlines on the internet. One headline from a financial advisor, Paul Mladjenovic, had a title that caught my attention. When I opened the link, it said he wanted everyone to consider three simple things to gain greater financial peace of mind.

1. Diversify away from paper assets.
2. Accumulate essentials
3. Refocus your portfolio with emphasis on "Human Need".

His second item coming from a non-Christian perspective really caught my attention. He said, "Accumulate essentials". He went on to say, "As odd as this may sound for some of you, consider starting a pantry or otherwise consider stocking up on essentials such as non-perishable foods, extra water, etc. NO, I am not asking you to become a survivalist or a hermit. I consider this to be just another form of diversification. The world is too precarious right now and is quite vulnerable to disruptions. Severe inflation is not far off. Potential problems can come from a variety of expected and unexpected venues. What do you think will have greater value a few years from now, a dollar or a can of soup?" I think this is sound advice for anyone. I could not have said it better.

3. If you are the pastor of a church you should consider starting home cell Bible studies or cell groups. I believe as persecution grows against the church and Christians, we will need to go underground. Already under our newly elected president, there is talk of eliminating churches tax-exempt status, and eliminating tax deductions for giving to churches and charities. If our country and the world go into a time of global economic collapse as we approach the Lord's coming, it is easy to see the high tax burden being assessed on churches will cause many to go bankrupt, forcing the church to move into homes. Also, home cells can be very effective in bringing the lost to a saving knowledge of

Christ. When things start falling apart in our society and our economy collapses, and when the government is not there to meet every need the people have, it will be the close friendships that will develop in the small group settings that will make your Christian friends closer than a brother and who will be there when we are in need.

I believe Pastors hold a unique responsibility to help prepare their flock for what is to come. Pastors should realize the church will be in for horrendous hard times before the Lord returns. I believe churches should lead by example and have a food pantry for the needy. They should encourage their people to use a portion of their resources to lay aside essentials for the hard times ahead. Proverbs 21:20 states, *"In the house of the wise are stores of choice food and oil, but the foolish man devours all he has."*

4. I believe in the years ahead, leading up to the return of Christ for his bride, the church, or better yet the saints in the churches, will be responsible to preach the Gospel to their lost or backslidden family, friends, and neighbors. We should have extra Bibles. I believe God's Word says there will be a famine of the Word of God in the last days and we should be prepared while there are no limits on how many Bibles, hymnals, and songbooks we can have.

5. Food storage and gardening: So much can be said under this subject. The Bible clearly predicts food will be scarce in the last days, and many will die of famine and starvation. I believe many Christians who have been told the rapture will come before the Great Tribulation starts will turn bitter towards God and the church. I believe they will be part of a great falling away. The Bible says there will be a great revival in the last days as well.

Esau gave up his birthright for a bowl of soup, and I am afraid many Christians who fall away in the last days will be the ones unprepared for a time of Great Tribulation. When they are offered an opportunity to buy into the system of the antichrist for food, they will succumb. Many Christians in America do not believe we will see famine on our shores. If this is what you think, you will be in for a big surprise. We are more dependent on our food coming from foreign lands now than anytime in American history. Not only does our food come from places like Canada, Mexico, and South America, but many of the local farms that produce the food for the local market have been turned into housing developments or Wal-Mart's.

I believe we need to learn how to grow food in our own gardens. Stored food will run out, but if you learn to grow your own food, you will have food for your daily needs. Most people have not learned how to raise their own food. We are too dependent on stocked shelves in our grocery stores. If you do not know how to garden, do not wait to learn. Start practicing now. **Do not wait until it is too late to buy garden tools, seeds, and other garden supplies. Remember; learning how to can your crops and having sufficient canning supplies on hand is an important part of having a garden.**

We should look at the Mormons. They have been taught to prepare for hard times. They are told they should have at least a year's worth of food stored for unexpected calamities, whether it is losing a job or widespread hard times.

Today with all the natural disasters and economic turmoil in this country and around the world, The Red Cross is recommending that we have seven days of food and water on hand in case of an emergency. If what you are reading in this study makes sense to you, then I hope you realize that

201

seven days of food and water will not cut it. How much preparation is necessary? This is something we need to seek God about and pray for his wisdom and guidance on.

Some Christians say the Bible says to "take no thought for tomorrow." Stop and think about this. There have been extraordinary times in history when these words did not apply. Before the flood, God prompted Noah to prepare. Read Hebrews 11:7 (NIV): *"By faith Noah, when warned about things not yet seen, in holy fear built an ark to save his family."* God showed Joseph, Egypt was to prepare during good times for a seven-year famine to come. There was a time in the New Testament when the Christians had things in common during hard times, but how can Christians share if they do not have anything to share?

Would not you agree the coming of the Lord with the catastrophic events leading up to Christ's return will be extraordinary times? Today, we are witnessing economic earthquakes that are shaking and taking down countries around the world. Millions are losing their homes to foreclosure. Many are losing all they have worked years to accumulate. I know Christians who are up to their ears in debt, trying to hold onto multiple assets and homes that are more than they can afford. Many are holding on tightly, hoping some bailout will rescue them. I am praying we will see an economic turn-around, and if this happens, I pray the church will realize we have been seeing the birth pains leading up to the coming of the Lord, and recognize time is short. We need to take the short time we have to consolidate our debts, pay off our home, if possible. Turn off the television and turn God's Word on in our lives. Let God show you what you need to do with the short time we have before his coming.

I want to encourage the readers of this book to consider obtaining a food and preparedness insurance policy. If you

202

buy a home, there may be less than one in a thousand odds your home will burn down, but you are required by the bank to have a fire insurance policy. If you buy a car and drive, even though the chances of your having an accident are less than one in a thousand, you are required to have an auto insurance policy. Now if you have studied along with me and agree we are seeing unprecedented times and cataclysmic events are sending clouds of uncertainty around the world, you must realize before the world or America will be willing to agree to join a one-world government, America will experience economic and social collapse. The will of the world to resist change will be broken. If you believe as I do that the odds of these things happening before the Lord's return are at least fifty-fifty, why not acquire a preparedness insurance policy? I hope your response will not be what I heard from one pastor, "Why store food or have a garden; others will only steal it from you anyway?" It is a good thing Noah or Joseph did not have that attitude.

In closing I would like to encourage you to start buying extra food items on a weekly basis. I find that if I shop the sales, when I see certain canned goods at a good price, I will buy ten instead of two. With frugal buying, you will discover you can accumulate quite a pantry without expanding your food budget. I recently figured out that for $300 you can buy enough food for one person for a year at a box store, (such as Costco) food that will store well for years. I'm talking about rice, beans, oatmeal, and other items to compliment a simple diet that will keep you alive on a low budget. If you have the financial resources you should consider buying food that is packaged to last from ten to twenty years or more. Again there are creative ways to find the money you need to make this type of investment. Maybe it is time to sell the boat, the motorcycle or some other cherished item that you will not need when your way of life has been turned upside down. Below I will list three sources for long term food. Realize that your grocery store is a good source as well as the discount box stores. I have read studies that have shown that regular canned goods stored in a cool place are still good to eat after thirty years with very little taste and nutrient loss.

1. Jim Bakker Ministries, They sell food packages that come in large buckets that are freeze dried products that will last for twenty years. I believe some of their packages are the best value per serving that can be found. You can contact them at; 417-779-9000. Their internet address is, www.jimbakkershow.com/shop

2. Nitro-Pak, This Company sells a vast assortment of food and preparedness products. They are distributors for the Mountain House brand of freeze dried food; this is truly the gourmet of long term food. This product is the same product that you buy in camping stores that you only need to add boiling water and in ten minutes your meal is ready to eat. You may reach them at 800-866-4876 or on the internet at, www.nitro-pak.com

3. Ready Made Resources, This Company is probably the biggest resource for both long term food and preparedness products that you could find. They sell packages that will be balanced with dehydrated, freeze dried and whole grains for long term storage. I have talked to the owner of this company and He is very much committed to helping Christians prepare for hard times ahead. You can reach this company at 800-627-3809 or on the internet at, www.readymaderesources.com

15. Closing thoughts about the Lord's return

The Bible says the weapons of our warfare are powerful through God for the pulling down of strongholds. In the last days, and I am talking about now, God is raising up an army. This army must not shrink back from the task ahead. God's army will be fully equipped with God's most powerful weapons, but if we shrink back, God is not pleased. If we do not appropriate the weapons God has made available, we will not be prepared for what lies ahead.

I remember as a teenager visiting the Winchester Gun Museum in New Haven, Connecticut. I was so intrigued to see the Gatlin gun. I still have a picture I took of this awesome weapon. The display of this weapon gave some background information I have never forgotten. It said this model of Gatlin gun was made available to General Custer. This gun could shoot 200 rounds a minute, and when General Custer received word he should take it with him to Little Big Horn, his response was it would just slow him down. So he went charging out to meet the enemy, and when he found himself surrounded, he must have thought, "I have two hundred Indians a minute more than I can handle. Why didn't I bring that gun?" Well, it was too late for him, at that point.

The Bible says the weapons of our warfare are powerful for the pulling down of strongholds. There is a weapon in the arsenal of God like the Gatlin gun, and it is often left behind. This weapon is prayer and fasting. I would like to share a couple of stories of how I learned about how prayer and fasting can greatly benefit your life.

205

Back in the early seventies, when I was saved, I was working in a logging camp for most of the year; then I would attend college in the winters. Before I attended Bible school, I was going to college at the University of Alaska in Fairbanks. While going to school, I attended Fairbanks First Assembly of God. I received some good teaching on prayer and fasting, and I started taking times to fast and pray while I was attending school. At that time, I did not have many struggles, but I sensed God was doing good things in my life. When I transferred to Northwest Bible College, after a couple of years in attendance there, I became concerned I had not met the woman of my life. So, before going back to college for my third year, I started fasting and praying seriously for God to bring that special person into my life. When I went back to Northwest College in 1977, I met Shawnette Rasmussen, who would later become my wife.

When I look back, I can see God's hand powerfully involved in bringing us together. Shawnette was six years younger than I, and I did not really want to pursue a girl this young, but God kept bringing her across my path. Before long, I had to ask God if he was trying to tell me something. I remember thinking that I needed to keep an open mind, as I did not want to miss God's will. God gave me many confirmations it was okay to pursue this neat cute girl. Before long, I had an opportunity to meet her grandparents, who drove down from Canada to visit her. They invited us to drive up for Thanksgiving, and God gave me special favor with them. When her parents got together with her grandparents for Christmas, Shawnette's grandparents could not quit talking about me. Then when I met her parents, when they dropped Shawnette off at the college after Christmas break, again God gave me favor with her Dad.

Our marriage has been good, and I would not trade Shawnette for any girl in the world. My point here is that I am totally convinced that Shawnette came into my life because I fasted and prayed. When I did my part to let God know that I wanted his best for my life, then God made all the arrangements to bring the most perfect girl into my life.

Now you would think that I would have learned a great lesson here, but the truth is, I hardly fasted after seeing God answering my requests from prayer and fasting. I believe I was just too comfortable. During the last two to three years I have rediscovered the power of prayer and fasting. As we have been seeing our country enter a period of economic hardship, I have been up against a wall financially several times. But for the last three years, as I have fasted and prayed for my needs and have sought God for his will in my life, God has come through every time. During this process of rediscovering the power of prayer and fasting, it is almost like I have rediscovered how great and loving our God is and how much he wants to have a close relationship with us individually. In these last days, we will have trying times ahead. We need to seek God like we never have before. As we press into God, we will discover how great and loving our heavenly Father really is and how much he wants to protect us and meet our every need. We must never lose sight of God's love for us. John 3:16 (NIV): *"For God so loved the world that he gave his one and only Son, that whosoever believes in him shall not perish but have eternal life."*

Imagine this; God is giving his church a last chance to finish the Great Commission and preach the Gospel to the millions who will be seeing hard times. As we are approaching the Great Tribulation, there will be many lost and confused souls who will want to know where to turn. Remember when 911 hit, and the churches were full for a week or two? When the Great Tribulation gets started, and the seals

207

start to pop open, the global events that will be taking place will make 911 and the twin towers look like a picnic.

Try to imagine the church being raptured just before any of this happens. On the following Sunday the churches fill up to overflowing, just like they did after 911. All these millions filling up our churches to get answers, and they are open to hear the Gospel. What will they find? All the pastors have been raptured and only the returning backsliders and lukewarm Christians are left to lead these millions to the Lord (the lukewarm Christians who have skipped out of Sunday school and have not studied their Bibles and do not have the answers). So, we have two scenarios here. We can hold to a pre-Tribulation rapture view and believe the saints involved in the war on the saints described in the Book of Revelation will be the ones the Bible depicts as the triumphant church made up of all the lukewarm Christians and repentant backsliders that were left behind but now are on fire for God. Those people would end up becoming the church tried by fire for which Christ is coming back. Or the second option, the rapture is a mid-Tribulation rapture, and we are prepared to help our unprepared family, friends, and neighbors, ministering to the needs of the lost and hungry, so that many will be saved, for we are still here and not yet raptured.

As I have said, I would rather see a pre-Tribulation rapture. It would be so much easier for me and all of us Christians. Wait a minute, does God's Word not say God is unwilling that any should perish? If the rapture is a pre-Tribulation event and it were to happen tonight while you were sleeping, what would it be like to stand before Christ, the one who gave his life that all could be saved? You have just entered the glorious gates of heaven; you have no doubt your eternity is secure. What would you do if Jesus were to ask you, "Did you do all you could to tell others about me before you left?" If Jesus could give you a choice to stay in heaven or go back and have a part in the greatest evangelistic opportunity in history, what would your choice be?

Another thought I would like you to think about is, God's Word says, "Christ will return for a pure bride, without spot or wrinkle." My question is, "Does this describe the church of today?" No, I believe the church of today is more like the lukewarm church described in Revelation. If you read in Revelation 2-3 where it describes the condition of the churches, the last church it describes is the Laodicean church. Revelation 3:15-16 (NIV) says, *"I know your deeds, that you are neither cold nor hot! I wish you were either one or the other! So, because you are lukewarm-- neither hot nor cold--I am about to spit you out of my mouth."* Is this the church today? I believe it describes many churches in America. I believe that if God loves the church in America or the world, for that matter, then maybe we need to be brought through trials and tribulations to wake us up so we become a part of the great revival that is spoken of in the last days.

I believe that if the church wakes up to the fact that they will not have a future secured by their retirement plans, our only hope is in Christ, and we are in the final countdown, it would lead to the greatest revival the world has ever seen. As the revelation of Christ's coming sinks in, it will finally hit home that only what is done for Christ will last.

I am afraid that the church of today is not ready for what is before us. When prophetic events soon begin to unfold and the timing of the rapture does not happen as we have been taught, this error will lead to great confusion. Many believers will rise to the occasion as Jesus' disciples did when given a choice by Christ to leave him. They said, "ONLY YOU HAVE THE WORDS OF ETERNAL LIFE". On the other hand, many in the church will feel God has abandoned them to suffer on the earth during this time, and their bitterness will cause many to turn away from Christ.

Please read God's warning to the church in Revelation 14:11, 12 (NIV): *"There is no rest day or night for those who worship the beast and his image, or for anyone who receives the mark of his name. This calls for patient endurance on the part of the saints who obey God's commandments and remain faithful to Jesus."* If you go back to Revelation 13, it talks about the saints being subjected to war on the saints by the antichrist. Then in Revelation 13:10 (NIV), it describes the imprisonment and killing of the saints: *"If anyone is to go into captivity, into captivity he will go, if anyone is to be killed with the sword, he will be killed. This calls for patient endurance and faithfulness on the part of the saints."*

If I am right in this study, that the church is to go through the first half of the Great Tribulation, we need to realize God does not want his church to suffer through part of the Great Tribulation for no reason. No! God wants his church to be a <u>victorious</u> church and to show satan his church will not retreat with its tail tucked in. No! We will rise to the occasion and do exploits for God, and in the end it will be satan who will lose. I believe we will be the victorious church God will use to reach out and snatch the lost out of satan's grasp. Every time we lead a lost soul to Christ, it is like we have punched satan in the nose. The salvation of those lost souls will make it worth any suffering we have to endure. Sure, we will have casualties, but we will win the war!

I was watching the movie "Titanic" the other day, and this spiritual thought about the last days came to me. I watched the minister on board moving among those who were not able to get on a lifeboat; these were people who knew they were facing certain death. The minister was not looking for a way onto a lifeboat; because, he knew he had a lifeboat in Christ Jesus. At the end of the movie, reportedly most of the lifeboats were only half full, and the fortunate ones who were in lifeboats could have gone back and helped those who were in the water drowning. This inaction led to a life-time of guilt.

In closing, as we are approaching the last of the last days, do we want to head for home with our lifeboat half full? Our reward is secure, so why should we be in such a hurry to head for home?

May we be ready for His Coming!

John Shorey

-

To order additional copies of this book

order online at
www.tribulationtruth.com

1 copy $14.99 each, plus $4.00 S/H

2-6 copies $14.99 each, plus $6.00 S/H

7-20 copies $12.99 each, plus $12.00 S/H

21-40 copies $11.99 each, plus $25.00 S/H

Thank you for your support to this ministry
John Shorey

If you would like to help me in the ministry of sharing the message of this book, please read the following page.

Now that my website is up, it is now easier to promote the message of this book. I would like to encourage you to help me get this important message out. I could not have published this book without God's help and the help of others. The website has extensive previews to allow people to see how important this book is. This site allows you to share this important message without having to loan or give out hard copies of the book. What I need you to do is call up friends and tell them about my book and give them the website. If you will encourage your friends to check this book out, I will trust God to do the rest. The web address is easy to remember and can be given out in casual conversation from home, work or church. May God richly bless you for having a part of this important ministry.

In His Service,

John Shorey

www.tribulationtruth.com